Country Roads
~ of ~
MASSACHUSETTS

*A Country Roads
Guide Book*

Country Roads
~ of ~
# MASSACHUSETTS

Michael Tougias

Illustrated by
Victoria Sheridan

Country Roads of Massachusetts
© 1992 by Michael Tougias. All rights reserved.

Published by Country Roads Press
P.O. Box 286, Lower Main Street
Castine, Maine 04421

Text and cover design by Edith Allard.
Library of Congress Catalog Card No. 92-081833
ISBN 1-56626-007-8

Printed in the United States of America.
10 9 8 7 6 5 4 3 2

Library of Congress Cataloging-in-Publication Data

Tougias, Mike, 1955-
    Country roads of Massachusetts / by Michael Tougias ; illustrated by Victoria Sheridan.
        p.   cm.
    Includes bibliographical references (p. 117) and index.
    ISBN 1-56626-007-8 (pbk.) : $9.95
    1. Massachusetts—Tours. 2. Automobile travel—Massachusetts—Guidebooks. I. Title.
F62.3.T68   1992   92-81833
917.4404'43—dc20   CIP

For my parents,
who took the time to show me
New England

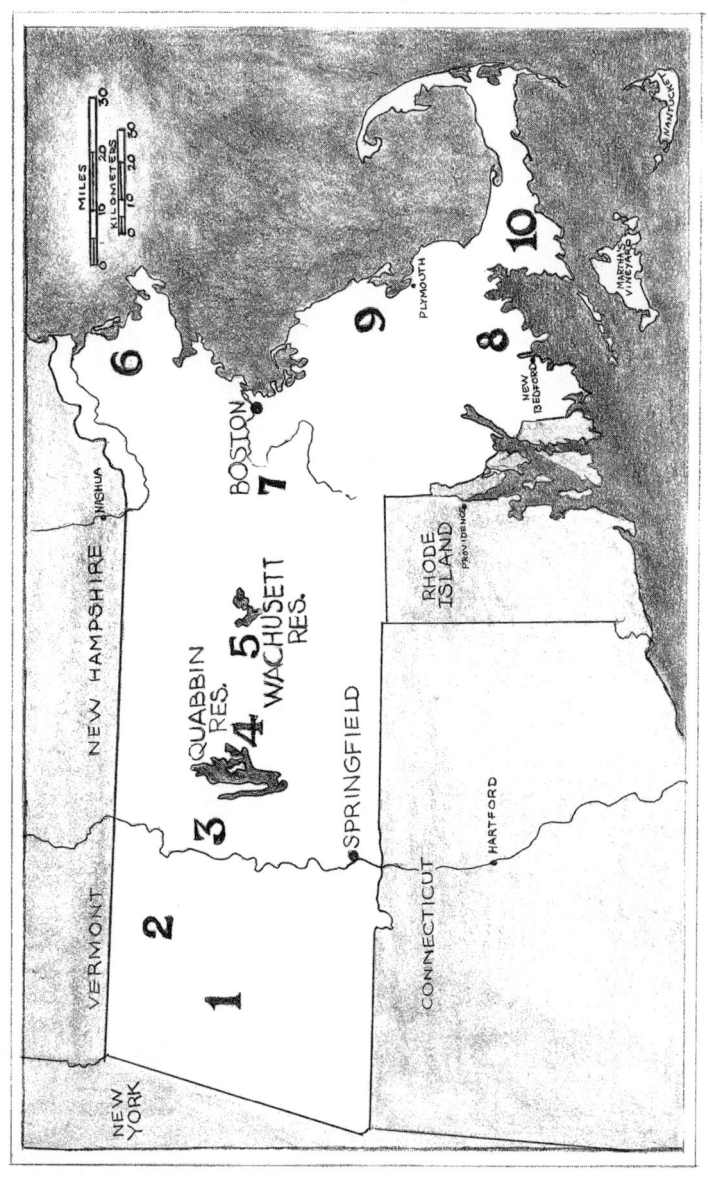

Contents

(& Key to Massachusetts Country Roads)

	Introduction	viii
1	Central Berkshires and Hill Towns of Hampshire County	1
2	Northern Hill Towns	14
3	A Connecticut River Drive	23
4	Quabbin Reservoir—Central Massachusetts	34
5	Wachusett Reservoir to Wachusett Mountain—North of Worcester	48
6	The North Shore	60
7	Discovering the Charles River—West of Boston	69
8	Cranberry Country—Middleboro to Buzzards Bay—Southeastern Massachusetts	79
9	The South Shore	93
10	Overlooked Mashpee—Cape Cod	106
	Bibliography	117
	Index	119

Introduction

Both visitors and residents of Massachusetts often think that you must travel all the way to northern New England to find quiet country roads. But green hills, blue rivers, and small villages can also be found in Massachusetts; you just have to know where to look.

Traveling the back roads, away from the crowds, has been a lifelong passion of mine. I avoid cities and well-known attractions, preferring the more rural roads where I find small adventures and pleasant surprises. Most of the tourists visit Boston, Cape Cod, and the islands; the rest of the state is somewhat overlooked. And although Massachusetts is densely settled, you can still find plenty of peaceful places to explore, even in the eastern part of the state.

Travel to a beautiful hilltop common in Princeton. Bypass Plymouth Rock and instead drive the country lanes to Redemption Rock, where Mary Rowlandson was released by the Indians during King Philip's War. Leave Rockport to the crowds and choose instead to wander up the coast a bit, taking a short walk through Stavros Reservation with its sweeping, spectacular views of the coast and islands. Central Massachusetts is perhaps best known for Sturbridge Village, but to really get a feel for the region, spend a day poking around the wilds of Quabbin Reservoir and the adjacent rural towns. In western Massachusetts, the Stockbridge area is always fun to visit, but *our* Berkshire tour explores the forgotten hill towns, far from the beaten path.

Introduction

These locations were selected for their scenic beauty, historical significance, and, above all, for their peacefulness. Along the way, stop at country stores, trout streams, old grist mills, apple orchards, and maple sugar farms: special places, rather than "attractions." Be sure to explore any backroad that looks inviting, but don't forget to bring a road atlas. I didn't try to cover every county in the state but instead selected my ten favorite areas from years of rambling about. Poking around is my speed of travel. Exploration should give you a sense of exhilaration and the thrill of discovery. You know you've had a good trip if you return home and see things with a fresh eye.

Most of the chapters include quotes from local people expressing their perspective on living in the country. I also include quotes from Thoreau because he so loved the wild places in Massachusetts. Thoreau was no world traveler; he found all the inspiration he needed close to home. We are fortunate that the state stretches out so far from west to east with incredibly diverse terrain, from the mountains of the Berkshires to the dunes of Cape Cod. Within this region are the villages and natural wonders that give New England its charm. I think you will be surprised.

1 ~ Central Berkshires and Hill Towns of Hampshire County

From I-91 take Route 9 west about 30 miles to Route 112. Drive south to Worthington. The trip makes a loop, beginning and ending at Worthington.

Highlights: *Sugarhouses, ski touring, Peru, wildlife sanctuaries, scenery, Crane Museum of papermaking, Wahconah Falls, Windsor State Forest, Kingman Tavern Historical Museum, William Cullen Bryant Homestead, trout fishing, fall color, pick-your-own farms.*

Mention the Berkshires and one thinks of towns such as Stockbridge, Lenox, Lee in the south, and Adams and Williamstown to the north. But not much is known about the small, rural villages tucked away in the center of the region. Our tour avoids towns and settlements of any size, preferring to explore where local populations are counted in hundreds rather than thousands, and there are more sugar shacks than restaurants. Bigger is not necessarily better.

The region is still unspoiled, with little or no commercialism—forests and farms dominate the landscape: a special place in a state as densely populated as Massachusetts.

Beavers, bears, deer, and otters have enough open space to flourish. Spectacular views will have you taking picture after picture, and the mountains have the power to invigorate. Much of the roadside beauty can be attributed to the sugar maples; they form canopies of green in the spring and summer, while in the fall their dazzling display of foliage is unsurpassed.

Maple sugaring is serious business in the hill towns of Hampshire County, and we begin our outing at The Red Bucket Sugar Shack in Worthington. Located just off Route 112 on scenic Kinne Brook Road, the Red Bucket has a gift shop stocked with maple products and an active sugarhouse. You can watch the syrup-making evaporation process while enjoying a breakfast of maple-topped pancakes in their small weekend restaurant.

Billowing clouds of sweet-smelling steam rise from the boiling sap and spread throughout the sugar shack. Freezing March nights have been followed by sunny days, with temperatures in the upper 30s, and the maple trees have responded. Here in the hills of western Massachusetts, the "run" is on, and the farmers have begun their annual sugaring.

From Kinne Brook Road, we travel northward up Route 112, passing Worthington Center with its 1855 Doric-columned town hall and English-style Congregational Church, built in 1887. Worthington Center is also home to the Country Cricket Village Inn and Restaurant, known for its Belgian waffles. A small gift and antique shop is housed adjacent to the restaurant.

Just a short distance up Route 112 is the Corners Grocery, which sits at a crossroads known as Worthington Corners. If you plan on picnicking, this old-fashioned general store is a good place to stock up. Constructed in 1860, the building also houses a tiny post office that was originally the only one between Northampton and Pittsfield.

Buffington Hill Road lies opposite Worthington Corners and leads to Hickory Hill Ski Touring Center. Here you will find over 650 acres of varied terrain where the trails are groomed and double tracked. The large barn has a cozy fireplace, and beginners can rent all the necessary equipment to get started. Call for trail conditions. Hickory Hill also hosts an annual Hot Air Balloon Festival, usually held in the late summer or fall.

Back at Worthington Corners, travel north on Route 143, passing by the ancient and handsome Worthington Inn, and then through some of the most beautiful scenery of the Berkshire Hills. On my last visit, I stopped at Karen and Bob Cook's small farm to tour their maple grove and small sugar shack. The Cooks welcome visitors, but be warned that the road to the house (Bashan Hill Road) can be tricky driving in winter, and their sugar shack is located 800 feet into the woods. Call ahead on weekdays. "The maple trees need to be about forty years old and ten inches in diameter before they can be tapped," said Karen. "It takes about ten gallons of sap to make a quart of maple syrup, and we burn almost twenty cords of wood every season boiling it down."

Most maple producers now use the more efficient gravity-flow tubing rather than sugar buckets, but enough of the tin buckets are still hanging to remind you of the old days.

Heading west on Route 143 brings you into the tiny town of Peru, population 650. Originally named Partridgefield, the new name was suggested by Reverend John Leland in 1806: "It is like Peru of South America, a mountain town, and if no gold or silver mines are under her rocks she favors hard money and begins with a P."

This is definitely a mountain town; in fact it's the highest town in Massachusetts, with an elevation of 2,295 feet. It is an isolated, wild kind of place, but one with simple beauty. The town center consists of nothing more than a small white church and the adjacent red library, which houses a tiny museum. The church is the highest in all of New England, and it is said that rain falling on one side of its roof finds its way into the Westfield River, while drops falling on the other side enter the Connecticut River watershed.

Peru was settled in 1767, and according to *A Bicentennial History of Peru*, the early pioneers chose this spot because of its

Sap buckets herald the maple syrup season

high altitude. "Fear drove them up from the fertile valleys of the rivers, fear of fever that lurked in the mist creeping through the lowlands at night. No less compelling was the dread of the Indians, who could descend with terrifying suddenness on the homes built in the shadow of hills."

On one of my trips to Peru, I stayed at a small bed and breakfast called Chalet d'Alicia, owned by Alice and Richard Halvorsen. The homey atmosphere and the remote location make this a good retreat for nature buffs who wish to hike the miles of state forest land or cross-country ski the old logging roads. Alice told me that they get "quite a few visitors who are simply looking to escape the city and get a little peace and quiet." To give you an idea of how high the elevation of Peru is, the TV at the Halvorsen's picked up stations as far away as Bridgeport, Connecticut, and Boston.

Much of Peru is designated as State Wildlife Management Areas, and the wildlife still has miles of uninterrupted wilderness to roam. I asked Richard Halvorsen what kind of wildlife he's seen and he chuckled, "Well, I stocked our pond with trout and then the otters came and caught every single one of them. Another time we had a bear come to our deck at night and break open all the bird feeders to get at the seed. When I told my neighbors, they said the same thing happened to them." Although it's extremely rare to see a black bear—they avoid humans—there are some big ones still left in the Berkshires. In fact, the state-record bear was shot in Peru and weighed over 500 pounds!

An interesting side trip from our circular route is to take the back roads down to Middlefield—provided they are not snow-covered. When the rest of the state gets a winter rainstorm, the Berkshires often receive several inches of snow. From Peru center you can take South Road (a real wilderness trail) southward into Middlefield. Along the way you will pass little-known Dorothy Francis Rice Sanctuary, which has six different trails leading from the small parking area. In the spring, wildflowers are plentiful, and summertime at the sanctuary offers tasty high-bush blueberries.

South Road leads into Middlefield Road, known as the "skyline trail," which eventually brings you into Middlefield center. Like so many of these hilltop villages, Middlefield seems like a town in Vermont's "northeast kingdom" rather than in Massachusetts. A church, a general store, and a few old homes make up this quiet country community. Inside the general store, a woman told me that Glendale Falls, located on Clark Wright Road, was worth a return trip in the summer.

At the crest of Town Hill Road, across from the store, there is a fine westward view. The road seems to disappear down into the valley, and I decided to follow it. After about a three-mile drive, I reached a lonely little hollow, where the road and a stream competed to pass beneath a stone arch bridge. I could only wonder what becomes of this passage after a heavy rain swells the stream.

Our tour now heads in a northerly direction, back up Middlefield Road to Route 8 and into Hinsdale with its Gothic library and Federal-style church. At the outdoor Stritch Sculpture Garden, located just east of town on Route 143, you can visit and ponder an unusual display of twisted metal configurations.

Continuing north on Route 8, we pass through Dalton, the largest town along our route. From June through mid-October, the Crane Museum is open, featuring exhibits tracing the history of American papermaking. The museum is housed in a restored brick paper mill located behind the Crane & Company office. It is open from 2:00 to 5:00 P.M. Monday through Friday, with no admission fee.

From Dalton we head toward Windsor along Route 8A and 9, making a stop at beautiful Wahconah Falls, located near the border of Dalton and Windsor. A path at the back of the parking area leads to the base of the falls. I visited here on a weekday morning in the late winter and had the place all to myself. Titmice, chickadees, and a lone bluejay flitted about, paying no attention to me as I poured a cup of coffee from my thermos and listened to the tumbling water. The water cascades down over a series of ledges, but only the final two feet were exposed; the rest was covered with ice. In some places, however, the ice was thin and clear, allowing me to see the sheets of water falling behind. We think of waterfalls as summer places, but I doubt the summer could match the beauty of the ice formation and the patterns of snow which lay on the surrounding hemlocks.

On that same trip I found more of winter's visual delights on a hillside along Route 8A in Windsor. The ice had formed a crystal coating over the birches and poplars, making them twinkle and shine. The dark green of the spruce trees helped make the picture perfect, and I stopped my car and walked up the open field. When I reached the trees, I could hear tinkling sounds from the ice as it lost its overnight grip on the branches. A set of fox tracks emerged from the woods in front of me and I followed them as they first went to a clump of bushes standing in the middle of the meadow and then wound their way down a hill and across the road.

When I think of that morning I spent following the fox tracks, I'm reminded of Thoreau's fascination with the animal: "His recent tracks still give variety to a winter's walk. I tread in the steps of the fox that has gone before me by some hours, or which perhaps I have started, with such a tip-toe of expectation as if I were on the trail of the Spirit itself which resides in the wood, and expected soon to catch it in its lair."

I tend to do more poking around and enjoy idle activities, like following fox tracks, in the fall and winter. These seasons have a calming effect, as you slow down your pace to match the earth's. When spring rolls around, the land awakens and my addiction—trout fishing—won't allow me to ramble. Instead, I make a beeline to my favorite river or stream. In the Berkshires, that usually means the Deerfield or Westfield river. Both are clear, icy-cold mountain streams that have native as well as stocked trout. Perhaps even better than these medium-sized rivers are the hundreds of small streams that carve their way through the hillsides. The trout in them are usually small, but to me the intimacy of working your way up the channel of a narrow stream is a total escape.

When I was researching this chapter, I used an old atlas I had owned for years. I was surprised to see the number of these Berkshire streams I had circled from past trips and the notes I had scrawled indicating the locations of the best pools. I remember one trip to the Westfield River on a hot August day when I caught absolutely nothing, but still had a fantastic time exploring its headwaters in Windsor and taking a refreshing dip in one of its chilly pools.

The windswept hilltop town center of Windsor is much like Peru—a post office, a church, and a library are huddled around a four-way intersection. Windsor, however, does have a general store, which seems to be something of a gathering place for the locals. When I stopped inside to inquire about road conditions on one of the side streets, the woman behind the counter said, "There's a few 'thank-you-ma'ams,' but you'll be all right." I couldn't remember the last time I'd heard that expression, but I do recall reading somewhere how humps in the road got the nickname thank-you-ma'ams. It seems that the horses pulling a carriage uphill would need a place to rest, and after passing the hump they could take a breather, using it as a kind of backstop to keep them from sliding backward.

You'll appreciate the nice view overlooking the mountains to the west just out of Windsor center on Peru Road, which runs alongside the library. Another interesting road to follow is Route 8A through Savoy, heading northeast. This will take you to the north side of Windsor State Forest, where a gorge known as the Jambs is located. Signs point the way to the forest via River Road. During the winter, River Road can be a bit slick, and you should take Route 9 east from Windsor and bypass the state forest until a return trip in the summer.

Windsor State Forest is a 2000-acre wilderness that offers picnicking, fishing, hiking, hunting, camping, and swimming. River Road is especially scenic, passing alongside the clear-flowing Westfield River and by a beautiful farm located at a bend in the river, just beyond the state park. In addition to Windsor State Forest, Windsor is also home to Notchview Reservation, owned and operated by The Trustees of Reservations. Notchview is located on Route 9 near the Windsor–Cummington town line. Like the state forest, Notchview is wild, rugged land, but it does have a self-guided trail that helps you to understand principles of forest management.

At the end of River Road, head eastward on Route 9 into Cummington. The Old Creamery Grocery sits at the junction of Routes 112 and 9. Besides groceries and other supplies, the store has a deli where you can order a sandwich and then sit at one of the three small tables in a sunny spot by the old stove. We will come back to this spot to complete our loop via Route 112, but first let's travel a bit farther down Route 9 into Cummington center by taking a left off Route 9 onto Main Street at the sign for Route 116. You might also want to travel up Plainfield Road, where the Swift River Inn is located. The inn was being completely restored in the winter of 1992, but the dining room and cross-country touring trails were open. A full restaurant, banquet hall, and conference center are also under construction.

Cummington is home to the Kingman Tavern Historical Museum. This jewel of a museum houses over 5,000 articles, reflecting a way of life spanning 200 years. The main building is the 1821 yellow house with seventeen antique-filled rooms. A replica of a 1900 country store has shelves filled with everything that would have been sold from 1900 to 1910. The store includes details such as a card tacked on the front giving the weather forecast as received by the postmaster and an old cracker barrel and checkerboard standing by the stove.

Adjacent to the tavern is an 1840 cider mill with massive wooden press and gears. Old hand and farm tools hang from the walls and ceiling of a nearby two-story barn. Inside the carriage shed you'll find a horse-drawn snow roller for roads, as well as a school bus on runners for winter use. The museum is only open on Saturdays from 2:00 to 5:00 P.M. in July and August, but appointments can be made for other times if you call ahead.

On one trip to Cummington, I forgot the museum was closed in the spring, but my trip was still a success because I met an elderly lady named Alta Bickford. Alta was 95 and had just received the "Golden Cane Award" presented to the oldest person living in town. I asked Alta her secret to such longevity, and she paused for a couple of seconds and then said, "In the country you feel the serenity of God. I take the time to watch the simple things, like the leaves coming on and off the trees and the sun coming up over the mountains." I then asked her what she thought of our society today: "I don't like so much importance being placed on money. If the people have money, they are becoming leaders and admired, no matter how they got the money."

Two other Cummington residents, Mae and Red Emerson, joined our conversation. Our chat turned to the Cummington of days gone by and Mae recalled the Great Depression: "When it hit, we never really knew it because we had always lived off the land." Red added, "I remember when we wanted water we would get a couple pails and run down to the well—we called it running water!"

We covered all kinds of subjects, standing there outside the Kingman Tavern Historical Museum. Later, driving home, I thought to myself that if the museum had been open I would never have met these charming people. Sometimes the highlight of a trip finds *you*, rather than you finding it.

One place you do want to find, however, is the William Cullen Bryant Homestead. This rambling country home can be reached by taking Route 112 south for about a mile and a half. Bryant grew up here, but his widowed mother was forced to sell the home in 1835 when she went into debt. Thirty years later, after Bryant had become a successful poet and newspaper editor, he bought back his childhood home. It is still filled with his personal belongings, books, and souvenirs from his journeys to Europe and the Near East.

The Bryant Homestead is my idea of the perfect country estate. The twenty-three-room white house sits high on a hillside, commanding sweeping views of the Westfield River Valley and the Hampshire Hills. Giant sugar maples planted by Bryant and his brother line the drive, which passes through open fields. The Homestead is open on summer afternoons, Sunday through Friday. From Labor Day to Columbus Day, it is open only on the weekends. Besides the house tours, you can take long walks or picnic on the surrounding 195 acres.

I love the quiet country crossroads lying below the Bryant Homestead where there is a five-way intersection. All of these narrow lanes are worth exploring; however, I'm partial to following Route 112 southward. It's a scenic road, passing through wooded hills and farmland. On the right-hand side, nestled beneath ancient maple trees, is 200-year-old Cumworth Farm. This is a working farm/bed and breakfast where people can visit the maple sugaring operation or pick their own berries in the summer. Call for picking conditions. Two miles further down, Route 112 brings you to Worthington Corners, where our "loop tour" of the Berkshires and hill towns is completed.

In the Area

All numbers are within area code 413.

Berkshire County:

Northern Berkshire Chamber of Commerce: 663-3735

Berkshire Chamber of Commerce: 443-9186

Bucksteep Manor B&B (Washington): 623-5535

Chalet d'Alicia (Peru): 655-8292

The Stall B&B Apartment (Peru): 655-8008

Canterbury Farm B&B (Becket): 623-8765

Long House B&B (Becket): 623-8360

Stritch Sculpture Garden (Hinsdale): 655-8804

Wahconah Stables (Hinsdale): 684-1178

Becket Arts Center: 623-5339

Jacobs Pillow Dance Festival (Becket): 243-0745

Crane Museum (Dalton): 684-2600

Notchview Reservation (Windsor): 684-0148

Windsor State Forest: 684-9760

Worthington Inn: 238-4441

Glendon Tree Farm: Choose and cut Christmas trees (Windsor): 684-3797

Blueberry Hill Farm: Pick-your-own blueberries and raspberries (Mount Washington): 623-5859

Ray & Marily Wiley: Pick-your-own blueberries and raspberries (Washington): 623-5859

Blueberry Heaven Blueberry Farm: Pick-your-own blueberries and raspberries (Middlefield): 623-5519

Hampshire County:

William Cullen Bryant Homestead (Cummington): 298-3239

Kingman Tavern Historical Museum (Cummington): 634-5527

Swift River Inn (Cummington): 634-5751

Country Cricket Village Inn & Restaurant (Worthington): 238-5366

Hickory Hill Ski Touring Center (Worthington): 238-5813, 238-5377

Red Bucket Sugar Shack (Worthington): 238-7710

Cook's Maple Products (Worthington): 238-5827

Cumworth Farm (Cummington): 634-5529

2 ~ Northern Hill Towns

Take I-91 to Route 116, exit 25, north to Conway. The trip begins and ends on I-91.

Highlights: *Burkville Covered Bridge, trout fishing, Chapelbrook waterfall, Pony Mountain hike, scenic small towns, sugarhouses, Bridge of Flowers, glacial potholes, fall color, craft shops.*

If I had the power to create and sculpt the land, I would mix a few flat valleys between gentle slopes and rolling hills. The hills would be forested with maples, beech, and birch to provide bursts of color in the fall. Hemlock and pines would be planted for their year-round show of greenery. Then I would include rivers and streams, ribbons of blue where trout would live. Some open land would be needed for contrast with the woods, so I'd bring in the farmers. Dairy farms, cornfields, and apple orchards would be scattered along the country lanes. Since I would want to live in this mythical place, I'd make the villages small and the people friendly.

Then I'd give my kingdom some simple name like Hill Towns. . . .

The little towns of Conway, Ashfield, and Buckland have to be the best kept secret in the state. Even though they are not far from Interstate 91 and Route 2, few people have heard of these towns, and fewer still have explored them. Perhaps that's because they don't boast any well-known "attractions." But they do have a rare commodity called space—enough to roam around enjoying incredible scenery and rural pleasures.

To reach these hill towns, exit I-91 onto Route 116 north. You will pass through the rich lowlands of the Connecticut River Valley and begin climbing into the western hills. Soon you leave Deerfield behind and enter Conway. It's hard not to notice the country lane on the left-hand side of the road, winding its way uphill toward a farm. This is Roaring Brook Road and it offers panoramic views to the north. It is especially scenic in the fall when the giant maples, which line the right side of the road, have reached their peak of yellows, reds, and oranges. Both Conway and Ashfield host fall festivals in late September or October.

At the corner of Route 116 and Roaring Brook Road is the Boyden Brothers Sugarhouse. I stopped in at the sugarhouse one spring afternoon and chatted with Mrs. Boyden, who was watching over the evaporation process. I mentioned that I had a sap bucket at home and wanted to try stove-top evaporation. She smiled and gave me a word of advice: "If you have wallpaper in your kitchen be careful; I've heard some real horror stories." I'm glad she told me that—my wife may not be ready for me and the kids to turn our kitchen into a sugar shack.

Continuing northwesterly on Route 116, you soon enter Conway. Park your car and take a walking tour of this fine old town. Tucked away on the right is the Field Memorial

Library with an unusual dome-shaped roof. Also on the right is the Conway post office, originally built in 1872 as the Methodist Episcopal Church. Where Route 116 crosses the South River, take a moment to look north (upstream) and you'll see a beautiful series of rapids as well as the site of the town's first gristmill, built in 1767. The mill burned in 1879 and was replaced by another mill whose remains are still visible.

It's possible to make a short circular drive around the center of the town by following the signs near the library for Whately Road and the United Church. This section of town is called Pumpkin Hollow and was the original village center. Go by the old United Church and then past a tiny triangular green separating quiet crossroads. Turn right onto Maple Street (near an old barn and antique shop) to complete your loop back to Route 116.

Heading out of Conway, be on the lookout for a covered bridge spanning the river. The Burkville Covered Bridge (also known as the Conway Covered Bridge) is one of only four historic nineteenth-century covered bridges in the state. Built in 1869, the bridge is no longer structurally strong enough to hold cars. It is open to foot traffic, though, and from the inside you can marvel at the craftsmanship that went into its construction. The Conway Historical Society says it is a "single span, multiple-king-rod truss arrangement" and is the last of this design in Massachusetts. Let's hope the state makes the commitment to restore it to its original condition.

We continue northwest on Route 116, as the road hugs the edge of the South River. I've fished the South River a couple of times, and while it doesn't hold large trout like those that inhabit the Deerfield River, smaller trout—mostly brook trout—live in the pockets of deep water. The stream is also stocked by the state in the spring.

Field Memorial Library, Conway

About a mile after crossing into Ashfield look for a sign on the left that says "To Route 9—Williamsburg." Make a left-hand turn on Williamsburg Road and follow it for 2.2 miles to reach Chapelbrook Reservation.

The waterfalls at Chapelbrook are quite beautiful, and you don't have to make a long hike to see them. They are located on the left side of the road, where the brook passes beneath Williamsburg Road. If you love waterfalls as I do, you will want to take a photograph of the cascading water framed by hemlock, beech, and maple. The brook can be further explored by walking the old logging path that follows the rushing water downstream.

Pony Mountain is also part of the reservation, and from its summit you'll have a tremendous view of the surrounding countryside. The hike to the summit takes about forty minutes round-trip, but is well worth the effort. When I climbed Pony Mountain, I felt an incredible sense of freedom and exhilaration from being in woods so wild and rugged. If only one could take a walk like this every day. Thoreau was a great walker, and in his essay entitled "Walking," he writes, "I think I cannot preserve my health and spirits, unless I spend four hours a day at least—and it is commonly more than that—sauntering through the woods and over the hills and fields, absolutely free from all worldly engagements."

A diversity of wildlife inhabits these hills, and on my visit I was startled by a ruffed grouse taking wing. Near the ledges of the mountain I heard a series of strange squawks echoing through the forest and later saw the "squawkers"—two jet black ravens. Bears also roam these remote forests, and many people believe there are still mountain lions here. Whether they exist or not, it's good to know that we have protected enough forest from development to make their existence a possibility.

Route 116 winds its way into remarkable Ashfield village, where just about the entire Main Street has been recognized as a National Historic District. It would be difficult to conjure up a more New England-looking village. The town has a general store, an historical museum, impressive old homes, and many historic structures. I even noticed an old hitching post on the right-hand side of the street.

One of the first buildings you see when entering Ashfield is tiny St. John's Episcopal Church. The church was built in 1827 and features Gothic pointed-arch windows. According to the Ashfield Historical Commission, "the square belfry, recessed slightly into the main block, is surmounted by a pinnacled balustrade." The other church in the town's center is the Congregational Church, a Greek Revival structure (1856) with a three-stage steeple.

The most intriguing structure in town is the town hall (1812) with its unique-looking steeple. The ornate steeple has "octagonal stages with balustrades, and [is] surmounted by a rope moulding." It was originally the town's second meetinghouse, and was moved to this location in 1856.

Try exploring Baptist Corner Road, an interesting back road leading into the hills northeast of town. About two miles up is Gray's Sugarhouse, where pancakes are served on the weekends during sugaring season. The sugarhouse and adjacent barn are quite picturesque, with a bubbling brook separating the structures. Some wonderful views of the surrounding hills await you just a bit further up Baptist Corner Road.

On one of my rambles to Ashfield, I stayed at the Ashfield Inn, a classic New England inn sitting on a hillside at the north end of the town's center. Built at the turn of the century, the inn's original character and elegance have been well preserved. It features eleven guest rooms, a large parlor with a fireplace, a cozy library, and outside porches—perfect for soaking up the country scenery. Owners Susan and Michael Brakefield made me feel right at home. The Brakefields moved here from Southern California to escape the ever-increasing development. "We fell in love with this house and the town, so we took a chance and made the move," said Michael. I've met many people like him—each person took considerable risks trading a secure career for a chance to live in the country.

Just beyond Ashfield, Routes 116 and 112 intersect, and we turn right onto Route 112. We are heading directly north toward Buckland, a secluded hill town that gets overlooked by motorists who zoom by on the Mohawk Trail (Route 2). It's the kind of old Yankee village that has dozens of narrow, isolated back roads with names like Hog Hollow Road, Apple Valley Road, and Moonshine Road. Best of all, the center of town doesn't even lie on the main thoroughfare, but instead is situated on a quiet lane high above Route 112. A small brick library, a white church, a post office, an historical museum, and some fine old homes are clustered together at the village center. A charming bed and breakfast called the 1797 House sits on the eighteenth-century crossroads in Buckland, right across from a tiny green.

Shelburne Falls, with all its shops, restaurants, and galleries, will seem like a metropolis after visiting tiny Buckland. To reach this unique village drive north on Route 112, and then bear right on Route 112 (also called North Street) just before the juncture with Route 2.

The Deerfield River dominates the center of town, which is fortunate, because without it Shelburne Falls' two most fascinating features would not exist: the Bridge of Flowers and the glacial potholes. The Bridge of Flowers is an old, arched trolley bridge that has been converted into a footpath lined with a wide assortment of flowers and bushes. It's a perfect place for a stroll in the warm-weather months—even at night when the bridge is lighted.

The ancient glacial potholes can be seen below Salmon Falls on the north side of the river. Cross the bridge and walk down Deerfield Avenue on the right. Formed during high water of the glacial age, over fifty potholes range in size from six inches to thirty-nine *feet* in diameter. They are beautiful creations of smooth, rounded rock with swirling shades of gray, brown, black, and white. The rock is called *gneiss*, a granitelike layered combination of volcanic ash and sand.

A number of artists and craftspeople live in the Shelburne Falls area, and some of their work is featured at the Salmon Falls Artisans Showroom. Pottery, jewelry, sculpture, paintings, weaving, and furniture fill the old three-story structure. It is located on the Buckland side of the Deerfield River, just a two-minute walk from the Bridge of Flowers.

There are dozens of other shops to explore. Be sure to stop in at Marty's Riverside Restaurant, perched above the river next to the Bridge of Flowers. It's a small country restaurant serving burgers, veggie sandwiches, homemade soups and salads, Mexican dishes, and fresh-baked desserts.

The easiest way to get back to I-91 is simply to take Route 2 east out of Shelburne Falls. But if you have the time, the more scenic way is to complete the loop by traveling back into Conway.

Years ago, I had heard of another unique bridge spanning the Deerfield River, far off the beaten path at the northern end of Conway. I recently called Bill Smith, an historic bridge specialist at the Massachusetts Historic Commission, who confirmed the existence of the bridge and gave me directions to this little-known spot.

From Shelburne Falls, follow the Deerfield River southeastward (past the Salmon Falls Artisans Showroom), traveling out of Buckland and into Conway. (The back roads get a bit confusing and it's best to have an atlas. My map shows the road leading from Shelburne Falls as Conway Street, which turns into Conway Road, and later into Buckland Road, then finally into Shelburne Falls Road.) After traveling perhaps five or six miles on these remote country lanes you will come to a sign for Bardwells Ferry Road, where you want to turn left. However, it's best not to make the turn here at this dangerous merge, but instead find a safe place to make a U-turn. Bardwells Ferry Road will bring you back toward the Deerfield River, first passing through forested hills along the South River and then through open farmland with nice vistas. The road gets narrower and narrower, finally bringing you to the old bridge in a quiet, lonely stretch of wooded country.

Bill Smith told me that this steel and wooden bridge is a lenticular through truss, built in 1882. "It's an amazing piece of work, the oldest surviving and longest of its type in the state," said Smith. The bridge was open to traffic when I visited, but I wouldn't drive over it—a couple of chunks of its wooden floor were rotted out. With a little imagination, you can easily visualize horse-drawn carts passing over this narrow bridge in what was probably an area of open farmland a hundred years ago.

To complete your loop to Conway center, simply follow Bardwells Ferry Road back to Shelburne Falls Road and head south.

In the Area

All numbers are within area code 413.

Franklin County Chamber of Commerce: 773-5463
Salmon Falls Artisans Showroom (Shelburne Falls): 625-9833
Buckland Historical Society: 625-6472
Ashfield Fall Festival (October): 628-3222
Apple Inn B&B (Ashfield): 628-4792
Ashfield Inn B&B: 628-4571
1797 House B&B (Buckland): 625-2975 or 625-2697
The Merriams B&B (Conway): 369-4052

Highland Sugarbush Farm (Ashfield): 628-3268
Purington Maple (Buckland): 625-2780
Mohawk Orchards (Shelburne Falls): 625-2874
E & J Scott Orchards (Ashfield): 628-3327
Covered Bridge Christmas Tree Farm (Conway): 584-8352

3 ~ A Connecticut River Drive

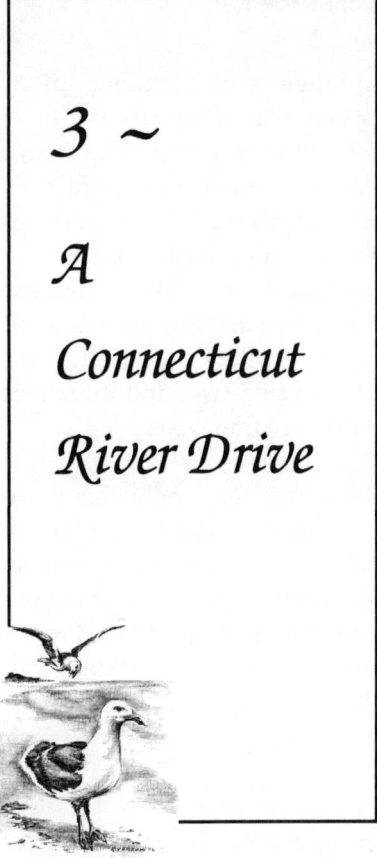

Take exit 21 off I-91 in Hatfield. Head east for a mile and a half, then follow the road north along the Connecticut River. The trip runs north to a point where you can take Route 2 back to I-91.

Highlights: *Wildlife along the riverbank—herons, ospreys, eagles, otters, deer; pick-your-own farms, Sugarloaf Mountain, Deerfield, Yankee Candle Company, fishing, canoeing, Northfield Mountain Recreation Center, excursions on the* Quinnetucket II, *a cider press, apple orchards.*

One afternoon in early October, I explored the Connecticut riverbank as I munched on my peanut butter and jelly sandwich. There were no people to be seen here, but rather odd-shaped tracks were visible in the sand. These "footprints" were larger than my hand, and I could see where they came out of the water and onto the beach. They reminded me of dinosaur tracks. As it turned out, the creature that made these tracks really does look rather prehistoric. The fresh prints could only have been made by a great blue heron, which must have flown away as I parked my car. Herons can often be seen silently stalking the riverbanks as they look for small fish or frogs to come within striking range. With lightning speed, herons snatch the bait in their long bills and swallow it head first. The great blue heron in flight is even more impressive than on the shore: its wingspan can extend to seven feet.

Walking along the shoreline revealed other bird and animal tracks. Far downstream some sort of hawk soared, making me wish I'd brought binoculars. I also wished I had my fishing pole. Although I'd never fished in this particular spot, I remembered as a boy going down to the Connecticut River after a period of spring flooding to find two- and three-foot carp trapped in tiny pools by the receding water.

The wildlife of the Connecticut River is only about two hours west of Boston. Once the western-most boundary of Massachusetts Bay Colony, the Pioneer Valley of the Connecticut River attracted settlers to farm the rich soil—even in the face of Indian attacks during King Philip's War and the French and Indian Wars. Despite its bloody history, something about this river gives the quaint villages along its bank a peaceful feeling. Perhaps it is because the people are so close to both the land and the river.

Migratory birds use the river as a feeding and resting area as they wend their way along the Atlantic flyway. The river runs 409 miles from the Canadian border all the way to Long Island Sound. Here you can sight great blue herons, ospreys, and even endangered American bald eagles. White-tailed deer and a host of other animals use the riverbanks as a kind of wildlife corridor, and of course, fish such as largemouth and smallmouth bass prowl its depths. By the thousands, American shad migrate upstream from the ocean every spring. Maybe someday they will be joined by the Atlantic salmon since efforts are under way to restore these magnificent fish to the Connecticut.

Farms with corn, tobacco, potatoes, onions, pumpkins, and peppers appear with more frequency as you follow the

River Road north. Barns and tobacco sheds dot the rolling fields. About two miles down River Road a small dirt road called Bashin Road lies on the right. Although it seems only to pass through the fields, about three-quarters of a mile down the road a turnoff takes you right to the banks of the Connecticut. A sandy beach stretches along the shoreline next to the slow-moving waters of the river.

After you explore the riverbank, head back to River Road (also called Main Street on some maps) and continue to follow the river north toward Hatfield. In 1675 local Indians attacked English soldiers garrisoned here. They burned homes and took prisoners in what came to be called King Philip's War, but the garrison held on. A hundred years later, farmers from surrounding towns met in sleepy little Hatfield to put on paper their grievances against the federal government. The discontent turned to violence in Springfield, where federal troops squashed the revolt known as Shays' Rebellion.

A couple of miles down River Road you'll find Nourse Farms near the Hatfield–Whately line. In the summer months, you can pick your own berries, but during my autumn visit I watched laborers harvesting live Christmas trees. They used heavy equipment to extricate the trees, then wrapped the roots in burlap and bound the branches for shipping. Buying a living tree to be planted after the holidays seems like an excellent way to enjoy this resource without destroying it. (If you live in the north, remember that the soil is frozen after Christmas, so your planting preparations will have to be made in November.)

As you make your way through Whately, more farmland lines the road. Near Deerfield, Sugarloaf Mountain juts up from the valley directly ahead. To reach the mountain, go left at the fork in the road; soon a sign welcomes you to Sugarloaf State Park. You can drive to the summit on a narrow road through a forest of white birch and hemlock. At the top you'll appreciate the breathtaking view of the Pioneer Valley and the river stretching far to the south. A checkerboard of green, brown, and yellow fields hugs the river while the mountains shine in their autumn colors. Almost directly below, the white steeple of a church completes this perfect New England vista. The high-rise buildings toward the southern horizon are not Springfield, but the towers of the University of Massachusetts in Amherst.

At the top of the mountain is a viewing platform, the site of the old Summit House built in 1864. Guests stayed at the house and danced in a large pavilion at the base of the mountain. In March 1966, the Summit House caught fire. Because of the snow, firemen were unable to get up the mountain to fight the blaze, and the house burned to the ground.

Sugarloaf Mountain is a great place to picnic during the summer when cool breezes pass over the crest. Picnicking is the best way to eat when you take a country drive since it allows you more time to be outdoors. Picnics mean you can eat when and where you want to. And one of the nicest picnic spots is the summit of Sugarloaf.

From Sugarloaf, turn left off the access road and go east on Route 116. You will see River Road on the left, just before the bridge over the Connecticut. The river runs right along the road here among dairy farms and fields of pumpkins. About four miles down is Pine Nook Cemetery, a rather forlorn-looking place in the middle of a large field.

As I explored the cemetery, where the breeze blew down this quiet valley, I felt a sense of peace. The river valley is so flat that for a moment it seemed I was on a Kansas prairie, half expecting a tumbleweed to blow by. But beyond the field there were mountains, and only maple leaves rolled by in the October gusts of wind. I found a number of interesting gravestone inscriptions from the early 1800s, one of which says,

"How soon this dream of life is over . . . we linger but a moment here." Another, written in 1816, reads:

> Friends nor physicians could not save
> This mortal body from the grave
> Nor could the grave confine it here
> When Jesus calls it must appear.

A little farther along River Road, I stopped to take a picture of a rustic-looking barn. At this point the traveler needs to make a decision to continue on to Historic Deerfield off Route 5 or bypass this section and cross to the other side of the river. If you have time, I recommend you drive the fifteen miles to Deerfield. But be aware that Route 5 is no longer a country lane, and tourists frequent this area.

Along River Road in Deerfield

To reach Deerfield's historic district, continue along River Road until it intersects Route 5, and then drive south among the antique shops, craft stores, produce markets, and restaurants. Signs will direct you to Historic Deerfield just off Route 5. This 300-year-old village opens a number of historic homes to the public. Besides the twelve original homes, many other old buildings and their contents have been brought to the site.

Don't miss "the door" at the Memorial Hall Museum—an original door that survived the Indian massacre of 1704. In its center is a rough hole hacked by Indian tomahawks. The Indians and their French allies shot randomly through the door, killing poor Hannah Sheldon cowering inside. They killed forty-eight other villagers that day and took at least a hundred captive.

During King Philip's War twenty-nine years earlier, Indians killed seventy-one soldiers in ambush at Bloody Brook near Deerfield. But the Indian effort to reclaim lost lands did not last long. Eventually the English gained the upper hand, and the native people of New England, the Algonquian tribes, lost their way of life forever.

On my last visit to Deerfield, I enjoyed fishing the pristine waters of the Deerfield River. Just a mile from Route 5, I angled for trout and smallmouth bass at a spot off Stillwater Road where the river makes a turn and flows north. The Indians referred to the hilly area blocking its path as Pemawachuatuck, "at the twisted mountain." Many anglers regard the Deerfield River as the best trout stream in Massachusetts.

Continue south on Route 5 to the Yankee Candle Company. This giant complex has candle shops, factory tours, and a candle-making museum. It even offers an opportunity to "dip your own" candles. Route 5 soon intersects with Route 116, and by going left on 116, you will have completed the Deerfield loop. Our drive now crosses to the east side of the Connecticut River.

A Connecticut River Drive

Immediately after crossing the river, look for Route 47 on the left, north through Sunderland. The first time I drove along here, I hit the brakes when I saw an enormous tree on the left side of the road. I realized it was a sycamore tree, by far the largest sycamore I've ever seen. In fact, I have not seen too many bigger trees anywhere in New England. As I walked over to this massive specimen, I thought of something Thoreau had written: "Instead of calling on some scholar, I paid many a visit to a particular tree, standing away in the middle of some pasture." The sign beneath the tree reads, "The National Arborist Association recognizes this tree as having lived here at the time of the signing of our Constitution" (1787). I walked down the road a bit and saw a homeowner raking leaves nearby. When I remarked at the beauty of the tree, she responded, "Yes, and it's messy too!" I'm sure I'd have said the same thing if its leaves blew into my yard.

Continue up Route 47. Where the road splits, take a left on Falls Road, which hugs the banks of the Connecticut. There are spots along here to park and explore the river. I took some snapshots, which I later copied in watercolor, of a blanket of yellow leaves next to the slow-moving river. A hawk circled above the river reminding me of a glider ride I took many years ago. With no engine, the glider must find a thermal to stay aloft, much as the hawk soars without flapping its wings on the uplifting draft.

Traveling up Falls Road to a right on Sunderland Road you reach Montague, a classic river town. (The roads here are confusing; check your atlas.) The Congregational Church, the post office, a Grange hall, the brick town hall, and a small village store surround a beautiful little common. It seems as if time passed this town by, and it is all the better for that.

Follow signs to Route 63 and head north. Farm stands along the road remind me that during colonial times this region was the breadbasket for much of New England. Although we New Englanders now import most of our food from other states, the Connecticut River Valley still contributes to city markets.

Stay on Route 63; it will carry you northward through the slight congestion of Millers Falls. If you are interested in canoeing or kayaking, however, look for signs for the New England Outdoor Center. The Outdoor Center has everything for the paddler, and offers rentals, lessons, and outings.

Soon after Route 63 crosses Route 2, a sign welcomes you to Northfield Mountain Recreation and Environmental Center, operated by Northeast Utilities. (Northeast Utilities uses the power of the Connecticut River to produce electricity.) This four-season center is a good place to visit, especially with kids. You can stretch your legs exploring the mountain trails by hiking in the warm weather and cross-country skiing in the snow. The center provides groomed ski trails, professional instruction, equipment rentals, and special activities.

You can also enjoy the center in a less active way by viewing the exhibits of the Connecticut River's past and present uses—such as ice harvesting, logging, and generating electricity. Or you might want to watch a film about Northfield Mountain or take a bus tour to the "powerhouse" cavern deep in the mountain.

Northeast Utilities also runs Barton Cove, located off Route 2 in Gill, a campground with picnicking, hiking, fishing, canoeing, and boat rentals. Bald eagles, our largest native bird of prey, have recently nested here in the only known nesting site in the state outside the Quabbin Reservoir restoration program, probably the birthplace of these parent eagles.

The increasing number of nesting birds and the sixty-one recorded eagles wintering in the state suggest bald eagles are making a comeback. As the northern lakes and rivers freeze in the winter, these migratory birds move south to settle on Massachusetts rivers such as the Connecticut and Merrimack. Bald eagles feed primarily on fish and occasionally on deer that have been chased out on the ice and killed by dogs or coyotes.

At Turners Falls, just beyond Barton Cove, a fishway carries anadromous fish (migrating from saltwater to freshwater to spawn) over the dam and past a viewing window. The facility is open during the spring migration when shad and an occasional salmon head upstream. It is best to call ahead for visiting hours.

Of all the activities offered by Northeast Utilities, the most interesting is the riverboat ride that cruises twelve miles of the Connecticut River. The *Quinnetucket II* excursion boat runs from June until Columbus Day, providing an excellent way not only to see the river up close but also to learn about its geology and natural history. Canopied with open sides, the boat holds sixty people; be sure to call ahead for departure times. (Quinnetucket, "long tidal river," is the Indian name for the Connecticut, and it's easy to see the similarity in the names.)

Just beyond the Northfield Mountain Recreation and Environmental Center is Neal Smith's Greenwood Farm. When I arrived Neal was in his cider house where the presses had been running earlier that day crushing apples into pomace. Neal said he grows "antique variety apples that few others bother to because they are so difficult to raise." He went on to add, "My farm is a throwback to the old family farm. I remember when almost everyone made apple cider and everyone's grandmother made apple butter." You can get both at Greenwood Farm, as well as pure cider jelly and pure cider syrup. I sampled some of this old-fashioned syrup and found it quite refreshing. The apple cider was among the best I'd ever had. Neal encourages visitors to take a stroll through the small orchard. Call ahead to find out when the presses are running.

In the Area

All numbers are within area code 413.

Northfield Mountain Recreation and Environmental Center (Northeast Utilities): 659-3714

New England Outdoor Center (Millers Falls): 659-3926

Yankee Candle Company (Deerfield): 1-800-243-1776

Historic Deerfield: 774-5581

Franklin County Chamber of Commerce: 773-5463

The Deerfield Inn (Deerfield): 774-5587

The Sunnyside Farm B&B (Whately): 665-3113

Centennial House B&B (Northfield): 498-5921

French King Motor Lodge (Millers Falls):659-3328

Choose and Cut Christmas Trees

Nourse Farms (Whately): 665-2658

Riverbrook Christmas Tree Farm (Whately): 665-3591

Maple Producers

Bears Maple Distillery (Whately): 665-3152

Brookledge Sugarhouse (Whately): 665-3837

Fairview Farms (Whately): 665-4361

Mt. Esther Sugarhouse (Whately): 665-4442

Pick-Your-Own Berries

Nourse Farms (Whately): 665-2650

Quonquont Farm (Whately): 665-3081

Clarence and Esther Warner (Sunderland): 665-3344

Blue Meadow Farm (Montague): 367-2394

Ripka's Farm (South Deerfield): 665-4687
Warner Farm (Sunderland): 665-3353
Tee-Zee Farm (Hatfield): 247-5244

Pick-Your-Own Apples
Clarkdale Fruit Farm (Deerfield): 772-6797
Quonquont Farm (Whately): 665-3081

Fresh Cider
Greenwood Farm (Northfield): 498-5995
Clarkdale Fruit Farm (Deerfield): 772-6797

4 ~ Quabbin Reservoir—Central Massachusetts

This trip begins on Route 9 near the Brookfield–West Brookfield town line, and describes a circle. Check your atlas or state map for the easiest way to get there from your starting point.

Highlights: *Memories of King Philip's War, Franklin milestone, small towns to explore, Quabbin Reservoir, Windsor Dam, the Enfield lookout, canoeing, wildlife, foliage, skiing, Petersham, Harvard Forest, Fisher Museum, Elliot Laurel Reservation, Hartman's Herb Farm, pick-your-own apples, country crafts, and old books.*

Huddled inside the tavern, the settlers could only wonder what the Indians would do next as musket balls and arrows rained down like hail. They soon had their answer: the Indians pushed a flaming cart to the side of the wooden structure, and in seconds the flames were licking their way up the wall. Using the last of their drinking water, the settlers succeeded in slowing the blaze, but for how long? The choice was awful: to stay inside meant death by fire, to flee meant being scalped and killed by the enraged Nipmucks.

In this siege (one of the first during the King Philip War) luck was with the settlers—a heavy shower fell and doused the flames. Shortly thereafter, soldiers arrived from the eastern settlements, and the survivors were rescued. The town, however, was abandoned and lay in ashes for eleven years, until 1686.

On Foster Hill Road in historic West Brookfield, a marker has been placed at the site of the attack. Viewing the actual place where a historic event has occurred is often better than seeing an exhibit in a museum. The small country villages west of Quabbin Reservoir are loaded with history, yet few people visit the region. Situated north of the Massachusetts Turnpike and south of Route 2, the area simply gets bypassed. Sturbridge seems to get all the tourists, leaving the Quabbin area as something of a hidden treasure.

Tiny village centers, like New Braintree and Hardwick, give one the feel of traveling back to the time when Massachusetts was still one of the thirteen colonies. Other towns seem frozen in the farming days of the nineteenth century, when families struggled against this rocky soil. Don't expect to see many reminders of the twentieth century—unless you count the enormous, man-made Quabbin Reservoir that covers the valley where four towns once stood.

Besides the King Philip War battle site, Foster Hill Road also features a Franklin milestone. Measured by Benjamin Franklin, the stones were set along the Boston Post Road in 1763 when postage was paid by the mile. Park your car and view the marker on foot. The road is a great place to stroll, with its fields, handsome homes, barns, and a view of the surrounding hills near the Meetinghouse marker, which is cleverly set in an old stone wall. Foster Hill Road is located on the north side of Route 9 in West Brookfield (near the Brookfield town line, where Foster Hill Road becomes Old West Brookfield Road).

Our tour makes a rough circle of a large region, starting at Foster Hill Road. Heading west on Route 9, you will pass through the center of West Brookfield with its long, picture-perfect village green surrounded by fine old homes. On the east end of the green is another Franklin marker set in a large stone frame. The town library is on the right-hand side, on the corner of Route 9 and Cottage Street, and you might want to stop in and pick up a copy of a pamphlet detailing twenty-seven historical sites in West Brookfield. An old cemetery with the graves of early settlers lies just a couple of hundred feet down Cottage Street near the shores of Wickaboag Pond.

Less than half a mile west of the library on Route 9 is the Book Bear, a bookshop specializing in used, rare, and out-of-print books. The shop is open seven days a week from 10:00 A.M. to 6:00 P.M., and "also by appointment and often by chance." It's a fascinating old shop, and you can really find some great bargains, as I did with three very old American history books.

If all this book browsing builds an appetite, you may want to dine at the Salem Cross Inn, also located on Route 9 in West Brookfield. Be advised, however, that this is a very popular spot and reservations are recommended. The inn was built in 1705 and is filled with antiques. Even the cooking is done the old-fashioned way—meats are roasted over an open hearth and pies are baked in a 1699 brick beehive oven. Situated on a 600-acre farm, the inn's hayrides and sleigh rides add to the unique atmosphere.

To the north of West Brookfield are the secluded rural towns of Hardwick, New Braintree, Petersham, Phillipston, and Barre. These villages are blessed with having eighteen-mile long Quabbin Reservoir for a neighbor. Nicknamed "the accidental wilderness" because of the thousands of forested acres that protect the watershed, Quabbin can be viewed from a number of different spots. One popular viewing location is the Windsor Dam area, located off Route 9 in Ware.

Quabbin Reservoir—Central Massachusetts

There's no avoiding a bit of congestion in Ware center, but the trip is worth the effort for the panoramic vistas overlooking the reservoir at Windsor Dam and the Enfield lookout.

A visitors center is located at Windsor Dam and is open weekdays from 8:30 A.M. to 4:00 P.M., and on Saturdays and Sundays from 9:00 A.M. to 5:00 P.M. It offers maps, books, and aerial photos taken in 1930 before the valley was flooded. A video presentation features oral histories from former inhabitants of the flooded towns.

Completed in 1939, the reservoir covers thrity-nine square miles, and is one of the largest in the world. About 2,500 people were displaced from 650 homes located in the valley—the towns of Enfield, Dana, Greenwich, and Prescott were wiped out of existence to make room for the reservoir. Before the flooding began, 7,561 bodies previously buried in cemeteries in the four towns had to be moved to a new cemetery at Quabbin Park in Ware.

Hiking is allowed at most gates surrounding Quabbin, and it's not unusual to come across a stone wall or even an old road that leads into the reservoir. About two or three miles down the access road from Gate 40 (located in Petersham off Route 32A) is the old center of Dana, now just a silent opening in the forest.

Soaring bald eagles can sometimes be seen from Quabbin Summit tower or the Enfield lookout. In the winter, the roads above the southeast corner of the reservoir often attract a number of binocular-carrying eagle watchers who look for the birds out on the reservoir ice. (I've found these birders to be most friendly and usually willing to show you where the eagles are and let you look through their binoculars or scopes.) From the observation tower, Mount Monadnock and Wachusett Mountain are visible to the northeast, as well as Mount Tom to the west. The reservoir itself is fantastic to see with its many islands rising from the water—once the tops of rugged hills before the creation of Quabbin.

The wildlife at Quabbin is as diverse as anywhere in New England. Beavers push their way through the water with their webbed hind feet and use their broad, flat tails to slap the water in alarm. When threatened, they can stay submerged for as much as fifteen minutes. The flooded ponds created by the beavers attract a wide assortment of wildlife such as wood ducks and herons, which make their nests in the dead timber standing in the backed-up water.

Other animals that are often seen include white-tailed deer, porcupines, raccoons, foxes, and weasels. Bobcats, fishers, wild turkeys, and bears all live here as well, but these creatures are much more secretive and are rarely seen. Some people claim that there is even a mountain lion roaming these forests, but the experts tell us that all the lions in New England were eliminated over eighty years ago. People who are not familiar with the area say there couldn't be any lions left—but when you walk through the remote and wild forests of Quabbin you have to wonder. One plausible explanation for the reported existence of a lion is that the animal was illegally released from captivity and has managed to survive by prowling over a great many miles of territory on its nocturnal forays.

To reach some of the most quaint and picturesque town centers in the state, follow Route 9 back to Route 32 and go north onto Route 32A. A post office, an old-fashioned general store, two white steepled churches, and a town hall that looks like a church line the perimeter of beautiful Hardwick common. Every August the Hardwick Fair transforms this sleepy town center into a bustling hive of activity with lumberjack contests, art exhibits, dinner inside the town hall, 4-H displays, cooking and sewing booths, produce and craft sales, cattle, sheep and horse shows, and even an old-fashioned frog-jumping contest. The fair is usually held the third weekend in August; call the town hall for details.

Summer isn't the only time to visit these hill towns; fall foliage is spectacular, and cross-country skiing or hiking during the winter are good cures for cabin fever. Thoreau enjoyed the cold weather months: "In winter, nature is a cabinet of curiosities, full of dried specimens in their natural order and position. . . . Our hearts are warm and cheery, like cottages under drifts. . . ." But be warned that this hilly region often gets more snow than the eastern part of the state and is usually colder. The back roads are often snow-covered and slippery.

Hardwick General Store

My last visit to Hardwick was in February, and my hike was made more exciting by the sighting of a coyote. There was no mistaking this "little wolf" for a fox—it was much bigger. I followed the animal through a field, and it seemed more annoyed than concerned over my presence, as it occasionally stopped to look back at me. After my hike I stopped into the Hardwick General Store and struck up a conversation with a woman recycling her cans and bottles. I excitedly told her about the coyote I had seen, and she said with a smile, "I know all about them; I raise sheep on my farm." Coyotes had killed some of her sheep, forcing her to install elaborate and expensive electrical wire fencing around her pastures.

On another February trip, with the aid of a telescope, I watched seven coyotes travel single file across the frozen surface of the reservoir. They seemed to be in a playful mood, occasionally stopping to chase each other. Late winter is the breeding season, so perhaps they were in the mood for romance. The scene reminded me of something one might see on a remote lake in Alaska rather than in Massachusetts.

Hardwick has scenic country lanes heading out in all directions from the town center. To the west is Greenwich Road which leads to Gate 43, where boats can be rented from the Metropolitan District Commission (MDC) to be used for fishing the reservoir. Canoes are not allowed in Quabbin Reservoir, but this boat launch also has access into Pottapaug Pond where you can paddle a canoe. Pottapaug does not have the cold-water species such as trout, but large pickerel and bass can be found there.

East of Hardwick center is Barre Road, which passes through farming country and leads down to the Ware River, once the site of a major Nipmuck Indian camp called Wenimisett. You can cross the river and follow Hardwick Street a short distance through some open fields, many of which were probably farmed by the Indians. Contrary to popular belief, the Indians of New England were not nomads; they lived in permanent villages and grew crops such as corn, squash, and pumpkins. Explorers such as Champlain and Captain John Smith were surprised to see patches of coastal forest cleared and cultivated with rows of corn.

Another interesting road out of Hardwick is Church Street (also known as Upper Church Street), which runs southward from Barre Road to a hamlet called Gilbertville, where Routes 32 and 32A split. There's not much on this hilltop lane—which is why I like it so much. Gray fieldstone walls enclose farmland and meadows; the combination of open space and silence make it a good place to park the car and soak up the peacefulness on foot. I recall a spring morning when I took a long walk here with chickadees and titmice keeping me company as I inhaled deeply of the fresh, rich smell of earth.

Our drive heads north out of Hardwick and into Petersham. In the winter, your best bet is to stay on Route 32A. But during the warm-weather months, you should turn right onto North Road, which is just north of Hardwick common. Look closely on the left-hand side of the road a short way up, and you will see an old hitching post standing next to a broken-down fence. Follow North Road onto Spring Hill Road for a spectacular view of the Berkshires to the west. Along the way, many open fields are lined with miles of stone walls dug from this bony ridge of land; no wonder so many farmers moved to the western prairies.

At the end of Spring Hill Road, go left on Old Dana Road to the Raccoon Hill Wildlife Management Area, which has a tumbling brook and an old logging road climbing up the hill. Continue down Old Dana Road to get back on Route 32A, and then proceed north. You might want to briefly explore Glen Valley Road, located a short distance up Route 32A on the right. This narrow, hilly road follows the sparkling waters of the east branch of the Swift River, and much of the land is protected in its natural state by the The Trustees of Reservations.

Follow Route 32A north onto Route 32 north and into the center of Petersham. The town center looks like something Norman Rockwell dreamed up, and I fell in love with it on my first visit. The large common and most of the surrounding structures are listed in the National Register of Historic Places, and it has managed to retain its atmosphere of a nineteenth-century New England town. Some of the buildings are in the Greek Revival style, with white pillars, and others are constructed from stone and brick. In the center of the village green is an octagonal bandstand, still used for community concerts performed on Sunday evenings in the summer.

Stop in at the Country Store for a light lunch or breakfast in the dining area at the back of the store. Owner Chuck Berube features homemade soups, salads, and sandwiches, as well as ice cream cones. Chuck told me he visited the town a few years back and liked it so much he bought the Country Store. "It hasn't been easy," Chuck told me, "but I've had no regrets, and I'm doing exactly what I want to be doing. And Petersham is a real community, where people still help each other—if you've got a problem you can count on your neighbors." Chuck's store was constructed in 1849 in the Greek Revival manner and is stocked with just about everything a passing traveler might need.

Another reason Petersham is so unique is the abundance of conservation land within the town, including the North Meadow common, located just off the town common, a few buildings north of the Country Store on Route 32. Owned by The Trustees of Reservations, the property is ideal for walking, sledding, kite flying, and photography. The lower meadows display wildflowers and meadow grasses that attract a variety of birds such as meadowlarks and red-winged blackbirds. Near the one-room country law office of Aaron Brooks, built in 1825, a trail leads to the wildflower meadow and around a small pond. From here, you can continue on to the adjacent Brooks Woodland Preserve to enjoy the old-growth trees, ponds, wetlands, and boulders once used by the Indians to grind corn.

Winterwood at Petersham is an elegant sixteen-room country inn situated just north of the common. Accommodations are on the second floor where there are five guest rooms, each with a distinctive personality and professionally decorated. During the winter, you can have cocktails in front of the living room's large fireplace, and in warmer weather, you can sit out on one of the many porches. Call for information or reservations.

Just beyond Winterwood is the Petersham Craft Center, which presents gifts handcrafted by local artisans as well as workshops and lectures. The gift shop features jewelry, pewter, books, prints, paintings, wooden ware, pottery, textiles, stained glass, and cards. An antique shop sells furniture, glass, china, and miscellaneous items. The center is open April through December, Tuesday through Sunday, 11:30 A.M. to 4:00 P.M.

Still further north on Route 32 is Harvard Forest and the Fisher Museum owned by Harvard University. Self-teaching trails through the forest emphasize the present vegetation and the factors that have influenced its growth—such as lightning, fires, logging, disease, and browsing by deer. The museum features twenty-three, three-dimensional dioramas portraying the history of the woodlands, accompanied by an audio presentation that takes the visitor through a forest's ecology.

Our next destination is Phillipston, with a town center even smaller and quieter than Hardwick. It can be reached by going back south on Route 32 from the Fisher Museum and then turning left on Route 101, followed by another left onto Petersham Road. These two roads are quite rural, passing through thick stands of hemlock, pine, and maple. At the beginning of Petersham Road, I noticed a beaver dam, and I stopped to check it out. An old man was hiking down the road, and he told me he was surprised to see the dam, saying that it wasn't there a month ago. In just thirty days, working at night, the beavers had constructed a twenty-five-foot wall of sticks and mud strong enough to hold back the force of the stream.

It looks like modern time bypassed tiny Phillipston center with its half-circle village green dominated by the Congregational Church, built in 1785. The church is the site of an annual October pumpkin contest. On my last visit to town, I asked a woman working by the church if the building across the common was the post office. "No," she said with a smile, "but I'm the mail carrier." That was how I came to meet Nancy MacEwen, Phillipston's "post office on wheels." This charming lady took time off from her work remodeling the church's basement to give me a tour of this fascinating old church whose beauty lies in its simplicity.

We decided to climb to the belfry. As we worked our way up into the steeple, I noticed the ax marks still visible on the old timbers in the attic. Then I was truly surprised when Nancy showed me the wooden wheels of an ancient clock, carved by "Cabbage" Clifford over a hundred years ago. A 417-pound boulder was once the pendulum for this faceless clock that chimed the hours. The bells now chime with the help of electricity.

I took a few moments to stand in the belfry—the view was fantastic, and I took picture after picture. After all, who knows how long it will be before I'm standing in a church steeple again!

Before heading back to Route 32, you might want to stop at Elliot Laurel Reservation, where masses of laurel bloom in late June. Ferns and partridge-berry cling next to outcrops of granite ledge and lichen-covered boulders are scattered about the forest floor. The reservation is located off Route 101, just west of Queen Lake.

The final leg of our exploration takes us south on Route 32 and into Barre. Along the way you'll notice a scenic waterfall tumbling out of Conner Pond. Directly across the street is an entrance to the Swift River Reservation. If you like to walk, the reservation has a beautiful riverside trail that passes through an old-growth forest. A short distance farther south on Route 32, make a right turn onto Old Dana Road to see Hartman's Herb Farm, open seven days a week from January 15 through December 24.

Over 250 varieties of herbs are grown here along with many flowering perennials and assorted annuals. The shop features potpourri, herbs and spices, dried flower arrangements, wreaths, decorated hats, dolls, and other crafts. I also enjoyed strolling around the rustic grounds where goats, chickens, sheep, and rabbits were a big hit with two six- and seven-year-old visitors. Both the children and I spent a few minutes visiting with Pinky, a most enormous, friendly hog whose ears hide its eyes. The Hartmans also run a small, two-guest-room bed and breakfast from their colonial home in the country.

Back on Route 32, we travel through Barre center, home of the Colonel Isaac Barre Restaurant and Meetinghouse Tavern, known for its fine dining. Somewhat larger than the other villages, Barre has an antique shop and other stores to explore. Continue south on Route 32 and then follow Route 67 into New Braintree. Take a right turn off Route 67 onto Barre Cutoff Road and go left at the end.

The hilltop center of New Braintree is comprised of a church, an old cemetery, a post office, and a Christmas tree farm called Kip's. You can choose and cut your own tree or shop in the gift shop from October 1 through December 20.

West Brookfield Road, heading south from New Braintree, is a treat for the country road lover. Farms, meadows, mountain views, stone walls, and giant roadside maples make it a pleasure to drive or bicycle. When the road enters West Brookfield, it turns into New Braintree Road and eventually leads to the back end of the West Brookfield common, not too far from where we started this long circular outing.

Our final destination is Brookfield Orchards, situated in North Brookfield. To reach the orchards, travel east on Route 9 and look for the signs on the left-hand side of the road near Harrington Avenue. The Lincoln family has owned and operated Brookfield Orchards for three generations. They have about 200 acres of fruit trees, and harvest season begins as early as mid-July on some varieties. You can pick your own apples on weekends in September and October. Early May is usually the time to see the apple blossoms, which put on a fragrant and colorful show.

Brookfield Orchards is one of the few orchards that is open year-round. Their country store features jams, jellies, maple sugar and syrup, cheese, and a complete array of apple products. Kids will love the stuffed animals, indoor waterfall, and penny candy department, while adults will appreciate the antiques that hang from the walls and the "book nook" at the back of the store.

During the winter months the orchards are used for cross-country skiing, and trails for both the beginner and more advanced skier wind through the hilltop orchards and surrounding meadows.

In the Area

Brookfield Orchards (Brookfield): 508-867-6858
The Book Bear (West Brookfield): 508-867-8705

Salem Cross Inn (West Brookfield): 508-867-8337 or 867-2345

Quabbin MDC Visitor Center (Belchertown–Ware town line): 413-323-7221

Hardwick Fair (Town Hall): 413-477-6197

Winterwood (Petersham): 508-724-8885

Petersham Craft Center (Petersham): 508-724-3415

Red Apple Farm (Phillipston): 508-249-6763

Hartman's Herb Farm (Barre): 508-355-2015

Kip's Christmas Tree Farm (New Braintree): 508-867-2660

5 ~ Wachusett Reservoir to Wachusett Mountain:

The Hill Towns North of Worcester

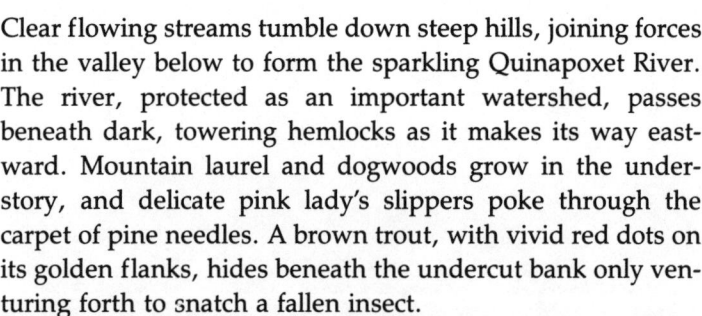

Take I-290 to exit 23. Take Route 140 north to Route 70 and drive north to Boylston. The trip runs north toward Route 2.

Highlights: *Mountain laurel and lady's slippers, Tower Hill Botanic Garden, Boylston common, Wachusett Reservoir, fishing the Quinapoxet River, Princeton, Wachusett Meadows Wildlife Sanctuary, Wachusett Mountain, Redemption Rock, fall foliage.*

Clear flowing streams tumble down steep hills, joining forces in the valley below to form the sparkling Quinapoxet River. The river, protected as an important watershed, passes beneath dark, towering hemlocks as it makes its way eastward. Mountain laurel and dogwoods grow in the understory, and delicate pink lady's slippers poke through the carpet of pine needles. A brown trout, with vivid red dots on its golden flanks, hides beneath the undercut bank only venturing forth to snatch a fallen insect.

The Quinapoxet River winds its way through the forest finally cascading over a small dam where it joins the reservoir to meet the water demands of eastern Massachusetts. Standing next to the shore, like a medieval castle, is the empty shell of an old stone church—a reminder of the valley town that was lost by the creation of Wachusett Reservoir.

These are some of the sights you will see at the beginning of our Wachusett region outing, a journey that takes you northward from the sandy shores of the reservoir to the windswept peak of Wachusett Mountain. Some attractions can be seen from the road, like the old stone church, while others, such as the half-mile boardwalk through a red maple* swamp at Wachusett Meadows, can only be reached by foot. Either way, the country beauty warrants repeat visits to these hill towns north of Worcester.

We start amid the vivid colors of the Tower Hill Botanic Garden, located off Route 70, about a quarter of a mile north of Boylston center. It's an appropriate place to begin because the hilltop property offers a sweeping view of the two Wachusetts—the reservoir and the mountain. Thoreau traveled near here, deciding to " . . . scale the blue wall which bounded the western horizon, though not without misgivings that thereafter no visible fairyland would exist for us."

You can get a fantastic look at the "blue wall" of Wachusett Mountain from the rocky overlook at the summit of Tower Hill. Pick up a map at the visitors center, then take a walk on the perimeter trail, passing through woodlands, meadows, and low-lying marsh. Along the way you'll find a wildlife garden, designed to attract an assortment of birds, bats, and butterflies. The walk takes about forty-five minutes, and benches have been strategically placed for frequent scenic resting spots.

*Here, red maples are the same as soft or swamp maples, as opposed to hard or sugar maples used for syrup and furniture.

At the end of the path, you are rewarded by the sight of a young orchard comprised of pre-twentieth-century apple varieties. Behind the orchard is the lovely botanical garden that is awash in colors during the spring. Hundreds of species of trees, shrubs, perennials, and annuals lie alongside the winding brick pathways and handsome stone walls. Although spring bloom is most spectacular, Tower Hill staff member Ginny Rich told me that the "gardens were planned for something of interest year-round. Even in the colder months there is still interesting color, such as the red berries on the shrubs, gold ornamental grasses, mauve-colored seedpods, and the various shades of green on the evergreens." Ginny also said the horticultural library, inside the main building, is the largest in central Massachusetts.

I've enjoyed the autumn foliage that surrounds the meadows in October and look forward to returning in the spring when the fields come alive with wildflowers and the 27,000 bulbs that were recently planted. Tower Hill Botanic Garden is open seven days a week, 10:00 A.M. to 5:00 P.M., but is closed on weekends and holidays from November through March. Picnicking is permitted, but leave pets at home. Call for more information on programs, garden tours, and special events.

Boylston common is just a two-minute drive south from Tower Hill on Route 70 (Main Street). The triangular common has a gazebo in the center and is surrounded by historical buildings. The one with the large stone blocks is the town hall, constructed in 1830 from Boylston granite. It is one of the oldest town halls in constant use in the Bay State. At the corner of Route 70 and Scar Hill Road is a private residence which at one time was Hastings Tavern. Built in 1818, it is an excellent example of the architecture of the Federal period. Next door to the tavern is a handsome building partially constructed of stones. Dating from 1904, the Sawyer Memorial Library is a fine place to spend a couple of hours browsing around. The library sells an excellent pamphlet called

"Historical Sites of Boylston" for those who wish to explore more of the town's back roads. The simple white First Congregational Church, standing at the top of the green, completes the ring of stately structures that make this town so picturesque.

Boylston has an even older town common, situated just a couple of hundred feet south on Main Street. The town stocks, used as an instrument of public humiliation, once stood at the edge of the old burial grounds (1745). The accused was placed in the stocks for all to see, usually with a sign around his neck proclaiming his crime: "B" for blasphemer, "D" for drunkard, and so on. These wooden structures had holes for the victim's legs, and sometimes for the arms and neck. A person might be placed in the stocks for as little as a few hours or for as long as several days.

Few towns are as lucky as Boylston in having a neighbor like the Wachusett Reservoir with its ring of wilderness protecting the water supply. Both Wachusett and Quabbin reservoirs were constructed to supply the Boston area's growing water needs. Twenty-five miles of surface and underground aqueduct connect the Quabbin Reservoir with the Wachusett, and an additional thirty miles of aqueduct carry water from Wachusett to Boston. In highly populated areas like Massachusetts, reservoirs are often the only places left that have significant tracts of forest.

By following Route 140 north, you will see the reservoir and get an appreciation for its size. Boats are not allowed, but Wachusett does allow shore fishing, and the trout and smallmouth bass reach enormous sizes in this deep, sprawling lake. A good area to walk the sandy shores is near the old stone church, located at the northern end of the causeway that separates Thomas Basin from the main body of water, near where Routes 140 and 12 split. Made out of great stone slabs, the church is a designated National Historic Landmark "to commemorate the town in this valley lost by the creation of the Wachusett Reservoir." Only the shell of the church remains, but it still has the power to inspire when you walk inside. The church sits in a grassy field at the end of a tree-lined path, with the clear blue basin at its back. Take a few moments to sit behind the church, soak up the sun, and relax by the water.

You can stroll the shoreline of the basin or cross the street and walk the edge of the reservoir. The size of Wachusett Reservoir and the many acres of surrounding forest form a unique environmental resource that attracts a surprising amount of wildlife, especially considering it is only about forty-five miles from Boston. Loons, coyotes, deer, bobcats, and even an occasional black bear are seen here.

The loon is a relatively large bird with a sleek, black head and black and white markings on its back. Its long, pointed bill is perfect for catching fish, which it hunts down by diving underwater, sometimes staying below for more than a minute. The loon's wings propel it beneath the surface and also in the air, where it can reach flying speeds in excess of sixty miles per hour. One reason you will seldom see a loon on a small pond is that the bird needs a large "runway" for takeoff—a sight to behold if you are fortunate enough to see it. Of course, the mournful cry of the loon is something one never forgets, and its wail is the very voice of the outdoors.

The coyote and black bear avoid man, and it would be rare to see either at Wachusett. I have yet to see a black bear in Massachusetts, but I once watched a coyote hunt the edge of a field at dusk. Both animals prefer to prowl at night and rest during the day.

After exploring the reservoir, it's time to take a look at one of the principal rivers that feeds it—the Quinapoxet. To view the Quinapoxet River, take a left from Route 140 onto Thomas Street and then a right on River Road, which parallels the river. A couple of miles down, River Road makes a sharp right-hand turn at a bridge. This is a good spot to park and explore the river on foot. Large granite blocks alongside the river indicate that a mill once stood here, perhaps to power a button factory (judging from the old steel buttons my brother found in the soil).

A trail follows the river downstream through a majestic climax forest of hemlocks and hardwoods. The pristine waters of the "Quinnie" are somewhat unusual for eastern Massachusetts, where most rivers are slow-moving and threatened by development. Trout are stocked. Each spring, anglers descend upon the river, some casting flies, others using spinners; and of course there are others who drift worms, perhaps

The Quinapoxet River

the deadliest method of all. More and more anglers, however, are realizing just what a special thing a clean, healthy river is, and they are letting their catch go free. Just to know the trout are here is enough for me; I often spend as much time listening to and watching the river as I do fishing.

The stocked fish are caught rather easily the first few days out of the hatchery, but it doesn't take them long to wise up, learning to avoid unnatural-looking food. Soon they are suspicious of everything—including sounds and vibrations—and only the stealthiest anglers will have any luck. The smart angler works his way upstream, knowing that the fish are also pointed in an upstream direction, where they cannot easily see or hear the anglers approach from the rear.

The next stop on our drive is the charming hilltop town of Princeton. It can be reached by a direct drive on Route 31 or by the slower, but more scenic, back roads. The peaceful and slow pace of Princeton reminds me of Mayberry, the fictional small town in the old "Andy Griffith Show." It's easy to imagine that life is simpler here where people still know their neighbors. Perhaps the reason for these impressions is the tranquility and beauty one finds at the town common; its high elevation seems more typical of Vermont than central Massachusetts. The last time I visited here I was with my brother Mark, an artist, who saw a potential painting from almost every angle of the green.

The white-steepled First Congregational Church dominates one side of the common. Inside is a beautiful old crystal chandelier, and in the steeple is a Paul Revere bell that can be heard from miles away. Two stone buildings occupy the highest side of the green; the one with the clock tower is the Goodnow Memorial Library and the other is Bagg Town Hall.

Over a hundred years ago, Princeton was a thriving tourist town with a number of inns to accommodate visitors from Boston and beyond. Evidence of those glory days can still be seen on some of the back roads, where a number of country mansions are located. The tourists don't visit like they did in the past, but they should—especially during the dazzling display of fall foliage. Peak colors, which usually last only five or six days, generally occur in mid-October. Orange, yellow, and crimson, set against a backdrop of evergreen trees, make this a photographer's heaven in the fall. While the roads leading to the White Mountains are crammed with "leaf peepers," sleepy little Princeton is quiet and equally scenic.

One location that shows color earlier than the hillsides is the red maple swamp at Wachusett Meadows Wildlife Sanctuary. This Audubon sanctuary can be reached by following Route 62 west out of Princeton, and then turning right onto a scenic country lane called Goodnow Road. Park your car in the lot, make a donation, and borrow a map from beneath a large sign. The Swamp Nature Trail features a half-mile boardwalk through wetlands few of us ever have an opportunity to see. High acidity, low oxygen, and fluctuating water levels in the swamp prevent many plants from living here, and some of the ones that *have* evolved and adapted are quite strange—like the pitcher plant, which captures and digests insects inside its leaves.

The red maple swamp was formed 10,000 to 12,000 years ago when the glacial retreat left behind a bowl-shaped depression where water accumulated. Red maples are one of the few trees that can adapt to the constantly changing water levels of the swamp. The bird and animal life, however, is quite diverse, with an assortment of snakes, turtles, and frogs, and a wide array of birds. Visitors may even be treated to occasional glimpses of an otter working its way through the water to prowl for food.

On the way back to the parking lot, the path follows an old section of Goodnow Road, one of the prettiest trails I've seen. It is closed to traffic, so you can follow the trail westward by foot and admire the stone walls, old-growth forest, and pastures in various stages of old-field succession. As you head toward your car, you can't help but notice an enormous tree growing at the edge of a field on the left. This is the Crocker maple—at least 300 years old and recognized as one of the largest sugar maples in North America. Walk over and sit on the bench beneath its branches and consider the visitors this tree has seen: Indians, colonial pioneers, and generations of farmers and their families. By the time the stone walls were built in the early 1800s, this was already a large tree, providing shade for cattle, sheep, and horses. Let's be thankful that this single tree was spared the ax; at least we can see what really old timber looks like.

If time allows, take a short (but at times steep) hike up Brown Hill via the summit trail. The top of this windswept hill is exposed bedrock, and it reminds me of being on the taller peaks in northern New England. Hardy, low-growing blueberry bushes are one of the few types of plants that can endure the cool, dry conditions of the summit. The views from Brown Hill are spectacular: To the north lies New Hampshire's Mount Monadnock, to the northeast is Wachusett Mountain, and to the south and west lie small farms, barely visible to the naked eye.

The final leg of our trip heads north toward Wachusett Mountain. From Princeton center take scenic Mountain Road. Large homes grace this country road, as does the old Meetinghouse Cemetery surrounded by a massive lichen-covered stone wall. The cemetery is quite distinctive; it lies at the base of a small slope and has handsome oaks growing among the headstones.

A few miles up Mountain Road is a sign welcoming you to the access road leading to the top of 2,000-foot-high Wachusett Mountain, the highest point in Massachusetts east of the Connecticut River. On a clear day, it is possible to see Mount Tom far to the west, Mount Monadnock just a short distance to the north, and Boston to the east. Migrating raptors such as hawks, falcons, and even eagles are sometimes seen following the mountain ridges on their seasonal routes.

Up until 1970 there was a hotel on the summit. But the mountaintop was totally isolated when Thoreau camped here with a friend in the mid-1800s. He recorded in his journal the pleasure he had on the trip, writing that the night was "so bright that we could see to read distinctly by moonlight, and in the evening strolled over the summit without danger." In a poem celebrating the mountain, he made this telling analogy:

> Wachusett, who like me
> Standest alone without society.

Wachusett Mountain State Reservation has over seventeen miles of hiking, cross-country, and alpine trails, and the chairlift runs year-round. I've enjoyed both night skiing here and hiking on an unnamed trail that passes through a majestic stand of old sugar maples.

Our final destination is historic Redemption Rock where, according to legend, the Indians returned captive Mary Rowlandson to her family. The huge, flat, table rock lies next to Route 140 and is now part of a small reservation owned by The Trustees of Reservations. You need a bit of imagination, but after reading Mary Rowlandson's account of her captivity, it was relatively easy to picture Indians gathered atop the rock, holding the captive and waiting for their ransom.

In 1676, during King Philip's War, Indians raided Lancaster, storming the Rowlandson house and killing or capturing the terrified settlers huddled inside. Mary was one of the lucky (or unlucky) ones who escaped death and was taken prisoner. She was forced to march west with a band of Indians from Lancaster (east of Princeton) all the way to the Connecticut River on a grueling journey spanning many days in the cold of winter. Rowlandson marched through the snow with a young infant (who died along the way) and little food or clothing. Later the tribe returned eastward, and she was forced to repeat the trip before her eventual redemption at this site.

In her book, *The Narrative of the Captivity and Restoration of Mrs. Mary Rowlandson,* she vividly details the attack upon her home: "At length they came and beset our own house, and quickly it was the dolefullest day that ever mine eyes saw. The house stood upon the edge of a hill. Some of the Indians got behind the hill, others into the barn, and others behind anything that would shelter them, from all which places they shot against the house, so that the bullets seemed to fly like hail."

Then she described what was happening inside the house: "Some in our house were fighting for their lives, others wallowing in their blood, the house on fire over our heads, and the bloody heathen ready to knock us on the head if we stirred out. Now might we hear mothers and children crying out for themselves and one another, 'Lord what shall we do?' "

Massachusetts is loaded with places like Redemption Rock—from the times of the Indians, through the American Revolution, and into the days of Henry David Thoreau. And best of all, the firsthand, eyewitness accounts are preserved in books available from any of our town libraries.

In the Area

All numbers are within area code 508.

Tower Hill Botanical Garden (Boylston): 869-6111

Wachusett Meadow Wildlife Sanctuary: 464-2712

Wachusett Mountain State Reservation: 464-2987

Harrington Farm Country Inn (Princeton): 464-5600

Lone Maple Farm: choose and cut Christmas trees (Princeton): 464-2476

Bayberry Meadow Tree Farm: choose and cut Christmas trees (Princeton): 464-2034

Bolton Spring Farm: pick-your-own apples and pumpkins (Bolton): 779-2898

Meadowbrook Orchards: fresh cider (Sterling): 365-7617

Nashoba Winery Orchard: winery and pick-your-own apples and berries (Bolton): 779-5521

6 ~ The North Shore

Take Route 128 north from Boston and exit at 15. Drive north on School Street in Manchester. The trip runs north from Manchester to Newbury.

Highlights: *Stavros Reservation, Essex Shipbuilding Museum, browsing antique shops and historic sites in Essex, Goodale Orchards, Castle Hill, Crane Beach, canoeing the Ipswich River, Topsfield Agricultural Fair, historic homes in Ipswich, Old Town Hill Reservation, Plum Island and Parker River National Wildlife Refuge, surf fishing for blues.*

In late October when the salt marsh was deep gold with patches of crimson, I visited Stavros Reservation. Dark green cedars mixed with vivid trees in orange, brown, and red to frame the wooded hill beyond. Far off in the distance the gentle outline of Hog Island rose from the blue Atlantic. No wind, no sound, and no movement existed except for a lone harrier hawk, wheeling and dipping as it hunted above the estuary.

Sandwiched between well-known Gloucester and Rockport to the south and Newburyport to the north are coastal towns still off the beaten path. Our exploration begins at the

The North Shore

Essex–Manchester town line and goes northward through Ipswich, Rowley, and Newbury. Except during hot summer weekends, when beachgoers descend on these towns, they remain quiet seaports that have not lost their country charm despite close proximity to Boston.

Exit Route 128 onto School Street in Manchester, where Agassiz Rock is located. This reservation features two huge boulders deposited here by glaciers. Louis Agassiz, celebrated natural history professor at Harvard, discovered the rocks and called attention to their geologic importance. Walk up a gentle quarter-mile path, which ends in a steep climb through hemlocks to the summit. The first boulder waits there atop Beaverdam Hill.

School Street runs into Southern Street, and that will take you into Essex center, once a prominent shipbuilding port. On Main Street the Essex Shipbuilding Museum features tools and materials used in the construction of thousands of fishing boats and schooners. One interesting item is the "scout horn"—a fifteen-foot pole with a leather pocket on the end to hold water—used to wet the hemp on the sails. Old photographs, drawings, and models round out the collection. The museum is open during warm-weather months. Whenever you go, take a moment to stroll behind the museum and visit the old graveyard, laid out in 1680, the final resting place of many Revolutionary War soldiers.

You can browse through the multitude of antique shops scattered about Essex, many of which are on Main Street, including the White Elephant next to the Shipbuilding Museum. Explore some of the old bookstores, seafood restaurants, historic buildings, and the site of the old shipyard on the Essex River. You can always ask directions if you get confused, although I remember inquiring how to reach the Museum and a smiling woman answered, "You know better than to ask a local about an historic site;

we never take the time to see what's in our own town." True enough.

Stavros Reservation is only a short drive north on Route 133 (Main Street) off beautiful Island Road. Because this narrow road offers excellent birdwatching, it's best seen on foot. Be sure to bring binoculars for birding and a camera for the scenery. A rustic barn on the left is framed by salt hay and stone walls; I guarantee you'll snap a picture. The other place to click your camera is the top of White's Hill at Stavros Reservation. This small drumlin, shaped by glaciers, is only 116 feet high, yet it commands spectacular views of Crane Beach, Hog Island, and Castle Hill.

Continue north on Route 133 into Ipswich; take a right on Northgate Road and then another right onto Argilla Road. Fields, woods, and farms stretch out on both sides of these roads as you head toward the coast. Be sure to stop at Goodale Orchards, where a wide range of farm products are sold in a quaint eighteenth-century barn. The apple and pumpkin pies are excellent. They also sell locally-produced honey and cheeses in addition to the usual fruits and vegetables you'd expect to find at a large farm stand. In the fall you can watch cider being made from a special blend of different varieties of apples. Children will enjoy the farm animals and pick-your-own apples, strawberries, and raspberries. To save this land from development, townspeople banded together and bought the Goodale Orchards in 1978. A year later they sold the property with agricultural restrictions to the Russell family, thus preserving it for future generations to enjoy. Call ahead to find out what's in season at the farm.

At the end of Argilla Road is Castle Hill, a fifty-nine-room seaside mansion built in 1928 by Richard T. Crane, Jr. This Chicago millionaire spared no expense in the construction of his "summer cottage." Here are crystal and brass chandeliers, woodwork from the Earl of Essex's castle in England, carved ceiling moldings, and many other exquisite features. Visiting Castle Hill gives you an idea of how the super-rich once lived without having to travel to Newport, Rhode Island. You can walk the grounds anytime except during private functions, and tours are given once in each of the four seasons. Call for more information.

Also at the end of Argilla Road is four-mile-long Crane Beach, a special place not just for summer swimming but also for winter hiking. Miles of shoreline stretch along Ipswich Bay with sand dunes, pitch pine forests, and a salt marsh. You might catch a glimpse of a white-tailed deer. Take precautions, however, to guard yourself against the ticks that may carry Lyme disease. Ticks are least active in winter, but give yourself a "tick check" after any walks in fields or woods.

In the summer, you'll find plenty of room to spread out and enjoy the surf and sand, but I must warn you of another problem animal, the biting greenhead fly, which is most annoying at the end of July. Equally annoying are the high summer admission fees; yet the beach is so magnificent that people are willing to pay the price, and the parking area can fill up early on a hot weekend.

For a change of scenery from the coast, consult your map and follow back roads through Hamilton and Ipswich that lead through bucolic horse country, woodlands, and small farms. One of my favorite places is the area near the intersection of Topsfield Road and Winthrop Street along the banks of the Ipswich River.

The Ipswich River winds thirty miles through wetlands dotted with small hillocks. Canoes are the best way to enjoy its beauty. Foote Brothers Canoe Rental operates from the banks of the river on Topsfield Road, and even a novice canoeist can try his or her hand with the paddle since the Ipswich is a relatively tranquil river. Foote Brothers will recommend an appropriate route. Have them take you and your

A country lane on the Hamilton–Topsfield town line

canoe to an upstream location, then let the gentle current and your paddle strokes carry you back to their headquarters. You'll have a good chance of spotting wood ducks and great blue herons as you silently round a bend. The river boasts trout, largemouth bass, bullhead, bluegills, and pickerel should you have the opportunity to do a little fishing.

If you wish to explore the river on foot, try rambling through the Willowdale Mill property, just beyond the Winthrop Street bridge in Hamilton and directly across the river from Foote Brothers. The large stone blocks of an early textile mill are still visible, as is the sluiceway that channeled water for power from the Ipswich River into the mill. Take a short walk down the path to the riverbank, where you can hear the soothing sound of the water pouring over the Willowdale Dam and racing downstream.

Topsfield Road runs west into Topsfield and east toward Ipswich. In October, inquire about the Topsfield Agricultural Fair, one of the oldest and largest in the country.

The English settled Ipswich in 1633. The Europeans, however, were just the latest in a series of peoples who called this land home; artifacts have been found here from the Paleo-Indian periods, dating back more than 10,000 years. The Paleo-Indians roamed this land during the postglacial period, when animals like the hairy, elephantlike mastodon lived. The terrain at the time resembled the far northern tundras, and temperatures were frigid for most of the year.

Ipswich may have more seventeenth-century homes than any other community. In the downtown area, the John Whipple House and the Thomas F. Waters Memorial Heard House are open to the public. My favorite historic place to wander is the burial ground dating from 1634. It stretches up a small hillside where beautiful sugar maples tower over ancient slate tombstones. It is especially beautiful in October with the maples a blaze of color.

To give you a sense of just how old these headstones are, consider that Custer's Last Stand occurred over 240 years after this burial ground was established. Some of the first names of those buried here—Jabez, Zerviah, and Mehitable—seem to have died out with those earlier generations. Climb the steep stone stairs up the side of the hill for a nice view of the western hills and Ipswich down below.

Continue north on Route 1A through Rowley, where residential areas give way to salt marshes, farms, and woodlands. Stop in at the Parker River Trading Post with its interesting assortment of antiques, collectibles, and fishing tackle. Soon after crossing the Parker River, pull over across from the lower green. This was once the center of the pastoral town of Newbury. A handsome monument, built by George Tilton of the Towle Silver Company, stands at the front of the green, and the old lower green schoolhouse is around back.

At the end of the green turn left on Newman Road, my favorite country lane on the North Shore. Giant maple trees, rolling fields, and the broad salt marshes of the Parker River watershed make this an especially attractive drive. As an added bonus, the Old Town Hill Reservation offers sweeping views of the Parker River and Plum Island. A short but steep ten-minute walk takes you to the summit of Old Town Hill. Enter by the trail marked with a wooden gate and sign. Although trees cover the hill today, in the 1600s owner John Kelly once killed a wolf among the sheep pastured here. A huge elm stood at the top, serving as a landmark for passing ships.

Another interesting walk from Newman Road takes you along the banks of the marsh to the banks of the Parker River. A green gate marks the trail on the opposite side of the street from Old Town Hill. Wildlife abounds here: great horned owls, red-tailed hawks, ruffed grouse, deer, and even coyotes. The coyotes have been expanding eastward over the past fifty years and are just becoming established in eastern Massachusetts. They will eat almost anything including white-tailed deer, if they can catch one.

Rather than head straight north on 1A, take the slower, more scenic back roads. Follow Newman Street through the marsh and then go right on Hay Street, which loops back to 1A. Just a short distance brings you to the Newbury town green with its tiny pond just big enough for skating in the winter.

No visit to the North Shore is complete without visiting Plum Island and the Parker River National Wildlife Refuge. To

The North Shore

reach this eight-and-a-half-mile-long barrier beach, follow Rolfe Lane to Plum Island Turnpike and go right. The wildlife refuge now owns two-thirds of the island; the other third is private homes and cottages along a wide, sandy beach. Swimmers should beware of the strong surf and undertow.

At the northern end of the island, where the Merrimack River meets the ocean, you'll discover a rock jetty that usually has a few anglers casting into the river mouth. The beach itself is known for good surf fishing, but I can tell you from experience, it's very sporadic. Stop at Surfland Bait and Tackle for the latest conditions. Evenings and nights are best if you're going after striped bass, and although bluefish have been known to blitz the shore at any time, your best bet to catch them is at dawn or dusk. A large-scale bluefish feeding frenzy is an awesome sight. The blues chase the baitfish toward shore, corralling the fleeing prey against the shoreline, where all hell breaks loose. While the baitfish are breaking the water's surface, the blues are just below, chopping away with their razor-sharp teeth. For anglers, there is no better time than a blitz: The blues are concentrated and will strike at almost anything in their path.

Parker River National Wildlife Refuge is one of the best birding spots in the northeast. Birds of all types stop here to feed and rest as they travel the Atlantic flyway. Birders should come early in the day or off-season since the parking areas are small. One winter I saw a huge buck standing atop a sand dune at sundown, and another time, a snowy owl resting far out in the tidal marsh.

First-time visitors should walk the various boardwalks to the shore or try Hellcat Swamp Nature Trail at parking lot 4. Climb the observation tower to get a panoramic view of ocean, marsh, dunes, and woods. The trail itself runs for about two miles over gentle terrain and takes about an hour to walk. Pick up a trail guide at headquarters.

In the Area

All numbers are within area code 508.

North of Boston Convention and Visitors Council: 745-2268
Essex Shipbuilding Museum (Essex): 768-7541
The Trustees of Reservations: 921-1944
Goodale Orchards (Ipswich): 356-5366
Castle Hill (Ipswich): 356-4351
Foote Brothers Canoe Rental (Ipswich): 356-9771
Parker River National Wildlife Refuge (town?): 465-5753
Air Plum Island (sightseeing rides, seasonal): 462-2114
Topsfield Fair (Topsfield town hall): 887-8571

7 ~ Discovering the Upper Charles River

Take Route 16 from Route 128 and drive through Wellesley to the Elm Bank Reservation. This trip describes a circle.

Highlights: *A bucolic trip along the Charles in the Boston suburbs. Canoeing, fall color, hikes, wildlife, South Natick, the Audubon Society's Broadmoor Wildlife Sanctuary, Millis historic trail, Noanet Woodlands, Lookout Farm.*

On the downstream side of the dam, a kayaker speeds through the turbulent water. Over the sound of the river I can hear him shout as he successfully navigates one hanging gate after another before the current pulls him around the bend and out of sight.

Above the dam, the scene is quite different—large coves sprawl out in different directions and the water's surface is placid with no visible current. A lone canoeist interrupts his strokes to lift his binoculars and examine the far shore for herons, turtles, muskrats, raccoons, or river otters.

The Charles is not just a city river. Here in the western suburbs, it's possible to see canoeists and kayakers enjoying the river in a peaceful country setting only a half-hour's drive from Boston. Not many major suburban areas can boast such a diverse natural resource lying so close to a population of over a million people. But thankfully, much of the land surrounding the Upper Charles is conservation land, where the nearby roadways give you a taste of old New England. From Needham to Medfield, no fewer than seven wildlife reservations abut the river. The area fits neatly into two U.S. Geological Survey Maps—a small patch of Massachusetts that I've spent many years exploring. Sunday is the best day of the week to explore the Upper Charles. (Because many commuters live here, avoid traveling during rush hours on weekdays.) You may want to bring a good atlas to navigate the back roads.

Elm Bank Reservation is a particularly attractive spot where you can enjoy the Charles. Even a few of the manmade features found here add beauty, like the cascading water at the South Natick Dam. Elm Bank and the South Natick Dam are only a stone's throw apart, and that's where our Charles River trip begins.

To reach Elm Bank (open Wednesday through Sunday) take Route 16 west out of Wellesley. Look for a small blue sign on the left side of Route 16 just before entering South Natick. The reservation access road crosses the Charles and then makes a large loop around the open fields of this former estate. The road eventually brings you back to the Charles and you can park at the canoe launch. To explore the river on foot, follow the riverside path behind the iron gate.

The trail takes you beneath some enormous white pines to a wide sunny bank by the edge of the water. During the summer, vivid patches of purple loosestrife grow all along the river. It is a pretty plant to look at, but it causes serious problems throughout the state. Of little nutritional value to wildlife, this import is expanding and crowding out the more beneficial native vegetation found in the wetlands.

In the fall, the river blazes with color of a different sort. The swamp maples along the Charles explode into reds and oranges in September, earlier than most other deciduous trees. I've always been partial to swamp maples (or red maples) because they not only add early fall color, but they also brighten up the spring with their dark red buds and flowers. Found next to wetlands like the banks of the Charles, they can withstand long periods of flooding. Look for other interesting trees and shrubs at Elm Bank, near the center of the property where the closed mansion stands.

After exploring Elm Bank, drive the short distance down Route 16 to South Natick. Park your car and wander about the village center, perhaps stopping in at the old brick Bacon Free Library; ask at the front desk if the tiny museum in the basement is open. Behind the library lies a small park surrounding the South Natick Dam. In the spring, the rapids below the falls are stocked with trout. Anglers of all ages can be seen wading into the river hoping to catch their dinner. In Harriet Beecher Stowe's novel *Old Town Folks*, she describes South Natick: "It was as pretty a village as ever laid down to rest on the banks of a tranquil river."

South Natick is perhaps best known for its "praying Indian" community. In 1650, John Eliot, a Puritan minister and missionary, brought his Christian Indian followers to South Natick, where they established themselves on both sides of the river. The settlement was supposed to assist the Indians in making the transition to the white man's way of life. While not totally successful (these friendly Indians were treated badly during King Philip's War), the community did last for over a century.

From South Natick follow Route 16 westward along the river. About three-quarters of a mile from the South Natick dam is the mysterious "praying woman" statue. The statue stands on a large boulder on the other side of the Charles. Although a number of myths surround the statue, it was a gift given in the 1920s by Daniel Sargent to his wife.

In his fascinating book, *Blue Highways*, author William Least Heat Moon also traveled west on Route 16: ". . . a quiet road out of Wellesley, that ran through stands of maple, birch, and pine, down along brooks, across fens, down miles of stone walls covered with lichens." What he probably didn't know is that a back road, South Street, is an even quieter, more rural way to head westward. Look for this narrow road on the left, a short distance from the South Natick Dam and the praying woman statue.

The stone walls along South Street—the snug fit of the boulders, their various shades of gray, and the giant maples growing next to them—are worth stopping to admire. The Massachusetts Audubon Society's Broadmoor Wildlife Sanctuary owns much of the land here. The entrance to the 600-acre sanctuary is on Route 16, just a short drive west of the South Street turnoff.

You can view the site of an historic gristmill at Broadmoor, where the giant stone grist wheel lies next to the stream that supplied the power. Visitors who arrive at the sanctuary in the morning might see white-tailed deer, which use the woodlands along the Charles as their travel lanes. Other creatures that also live here include foxes, rabbits, meadow voles, owls, wood ducks, and pileated woodpeckers —rather uncommon and a special treat to see.

In 1992, I was walking at the west end of the property when I noticed that Indian Brook had been dammed with sticks, vegetation, and mud. I had never seen a beaver anywhere in the Charles River watershed, but Elissa Landre, director of Broadmoor, told me that the beavers had moved in a couple of years earlier and seemed to be doing well. I asked her if she had located their hut. Landre responded that these were bank beavers, members of the same species that prefer to make their homes by burrowing into the stream or riverbanks. "I've only seen one of them, and that was at dusk," she added. Don't expect to see one of these nocturnal creatures on your visit, but it's still good to know the industrious beaver has once again returned to the Charles.

Tall white pines create a tunnel of green at the other end of South Street in the town of Sherborn. This affluent suburb of Boston is known for its handsome estates, horses, and acres of woodlands. A conservation-minded town, Sherborn has left a great many acres in their natural state, making it popular for bicyclists, hikers, and canoeists.

Turn left on Farm Road at the end of South Street. You will pass rolling fields and a farm that is quintessential New England. Even during the winter, you can often see huge flocks of Canada geese in these pastures. Many geese no longer migrate south, preferring instead to tough out the cold weather in open meadows or on golf course fairways. The last few winters in New England have been warmer than normal and this may have something to do with their new wintering habit.

Another creature living along the river is much less welcomed by farmers than geese. Coyotes have recently established themselves along the Charles, where they have killed more than a few sheep at nearby farms. These elusive, wily animals are here to stay. As troublesome as the coyote may be, there is a certain satisfaction in knowing that such diverse wildlife can be found so close to Boston. However, not everyone agrees; some argue that the coyote will upset the ecological balance that has evolved over the last 200 years. The red fox will probably be the biggest loser, as the larger coyote takes over its range.

A tiny old cemetery nestles beneath the pines and hemlocks on the left-hand side of Farm Road. In fact, the cemetery is so small, I'm sure some drivers have gone right by, never realizing it's there. I enjoy reading the inscriptions on the headstones, seeking to decipher a bit of the past from their words.

Continue down Farm Road until you come to the bridge with wooden side rails and granite posts. Park in the canoe-launching lot on the other side of the Charles and walk up to the bridge for a view of the river. Canoeists who head downstream pass along the property of Peters Reservation before

A fisherman enjoying the Charles River

entering South Natick. You can take a stroll through Peters Reservation by following the trail at the rear of the parking lot. A short distance upstream lies Rocky Narrows, one of the few areas on the Charles where the river narrows as it passes between steep, forested banks. You can reach the reservation on the northwest side of the river only by canoe.

I canoed through the Narrows after the heavy rains of Hurricane Bob in 1991, taking a newspaper reporter upstream for a canoe ride to promote my new book, *The Hidden Charles*. When we reached the confines of the Narrows, the water was flowing so rapidly we could barely make headway against the current. I've never capsized in a canoe, and I especially didn't need to at this particular moment—not with a reporter as my passenger. (I could see the story's heading: "Author spills reporter into Hidden Charles.") The fear of embarrassment, more than the threat of a dunking, gave me a shot of adrenaline, just enough to put a little something extra in my strokes to get us through that patch of churning water.

Continue your drive by going back across the river and up Farm Road. Turn left onto Forest Street just before the little graveyard mentioned earlier. This narrow country lane is popular with bicyclists, so please go slowly. Take a left onto Snow Street, then left again on Route 27, and finally right on Route 115.

The town of Millis has done something I wish every town would do—laid out an "historical trail"—mostly along Route 115. Follow the historical trail sign to South End Pond. During King Philip's War, nine families gathered at a stone garrison located here for protection against the attacking Indians. Also in the area (but on private land) are a series of mysterious trenches said to predate the colonists. The mystery has never been solved; some historians theorize they were made by the Vikings, while others think they are the work of ancient Indians.

South End Pond is actually connected to the Charles via Bogastow Brook, which spills into the pond at the south end and exits into the river on the northeast side. I've often launched my canoe at the pond and followed the brook into the huge Medfield–Millis marsh that borders the Charles.

Farther down Route 115, you can see more historic sites including homes from the eighteenth and nineteenth centuries. The Richardson House had a tunnel leading from the home to the woods. The Millis Historical Society thinks it was used either as an escape route in case of Indian attack or perhaps built later as a station for the Underground Railroad. Also on Route 115 is Oak Grove Farm, where you can walk the fields and woods of this historic site or, if you are traveling with children, use the small playground.

The second half of our drive, which follows the river back dowstream, begins where Route 115 intersects Route 109. On weekends, you can rent canoes at the parking lot adjacent to the river at the Route 109 bridge. The Charles is calm here, a good spot for first-time canoeists. If you prefer to walk rather than paddle, The Trustees of Reservations maintain good hiking trails at Noon Hill Reservation and Shattuck Reservation. You can reach these two forested properties by following Route 109 across the river and turning right on Causeway Street.

Visitors short on time can get back to Route 128 by going east on Route 109. Along the way, just beyond Medfield center, you can see the tiny Peak House built in 1680 by colonist Seth Clark. Because his original home was reduced to ashes during a devastating Indian raid that destroyed much of the town in 1676, Mr. Clark received a payment from the colonial government to construct this "new" house.

Continue northeast into Dover, a quiet town with many good-sized wooded estates. At Medfield center, go north on North Street and then take Farm Street into Dover. Follow Springdale Avenue into Dover center and wander into Seasons Gift Shop or through old Highland Cemetery (1746). Just beyond the town center on Dedham Street is Noanet Woodlands with over 500 acres of woods and water. The reservation is one of the best in the Charles River watershed for picnicking and hiking. It's a relatively short climb from the parking area to Noanet Peak (387 feet), from which you can see the Boston skyline nineteen miles away. A brook and ponds once powered the Dover Union Iron Company mill located below the restored dam and waterfall. The mill operated from 1815 until 1876, when a flood breached the dam and destroyed the mill.

After exploring Noanet, exit Dedham Street onto Willow Street, which spans the river at Cochrane Dam. Kayakers often come to practice their sport in the rapid water below this dam. You can pull your car off the road here and walk down Mill Street for a better look at the river. Upstream in Redwing Bay, great blue herons wade in quiet coves.

Follow Cross Street (located off Willow) to a right on Centre Street and then left on Claybrook Road. Running parallel to the Charles, Claybrook takes you through a tranquil, wooded residential part of Dover. Claybrook Road ends at Pleasant Street, where you will see signs for Lookout Farm. Here you can purchase fresh produce or pick your own raspberries, strawberries, or apples. On autumn weekends the farm offers pony and hayrides for the kids.

Pleasant Street leads to the South Natick Dam—and our circle of the Charles is completed.

In the Area

All numbers are within area code 508.

Broadmoor Wildlife Sanctuary (Natick): 655-2296
The Trustees of Reservations: 921-1944
Lookout Farm (Natick): 651-1539
Rossi's Restaurant (Millis): 376-4995

8 ~ Cranberry Country Ramble

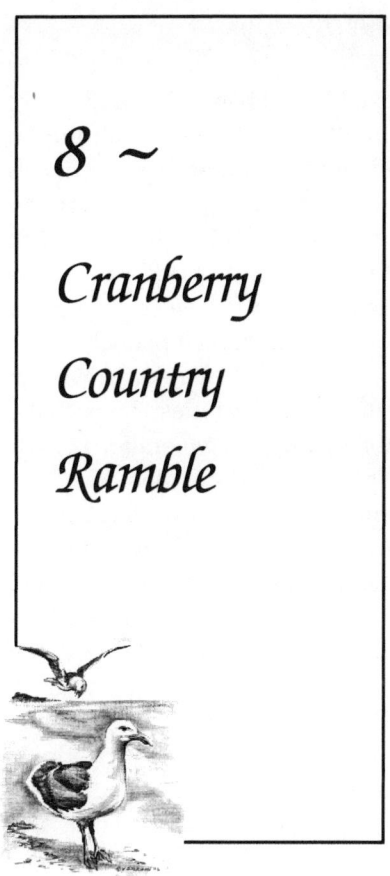

Take I-495 to exit 5. Follow Route 18 (running concurrent with Route 28) north. **Or,** take Route 44 west to Route 18 and turn north toward Bridgewater. This trip is divided into two sections: the first explores Middleboro, and the second, the small towns to the south near Buzzards Bay.

Highlights: *Titicut Green, browsing for antiques, memories of King Philip's War, Middleboro Historical Museum, Oliver Mill picnic area, Pratt Farm Conservation Area, cranberry bogs, Edaville Railroad, Cervelli Farm, Jonathan's Sprouts, Neds Point, Shipyard Park, Long Plain Friends Meetinghouse.*

Middleboro to Carver

A gray fox trotted along the edge of the old cemetery and headed for the safety of the nearby woods. It bounded over a fallen tree, stopping to glance back at me before vanishing into the undergrowth. Here in the village of North Middleboro, or Titicut Green, development has been controlled. Creatures like the fox still visit the outskirts of town, modern buildings have not yet spoiled the landscape, and the historic structures remain primarily intact. For a few moments at least, you can go back in time.

To reach Titicut Green, exit Route 44 onto Route 18 north, then take a left on Old Centre Street, followed by a right on Pleasant Street. When you reach the green, park your car; this serene little place with its historic buildings is best explored on foot: the Pratt Free School built in 1856, the old North Congregational Church with its wooden clock up on the tower, and the handsome structure on the western edge of the triangular green, the Federal Chamberlain School.

Under handsome maples trees, the Titicut Parish Cemetery includes a number of unique headstones. Inspect the interesting inscriptions memorializing past generations of settlers with first names like Zephaniah and Zebulon. The land where the cemetery now stands was a gift from three members of the "praying Indians" (converts to Christianity) in 1746. At least one of these Indians, James Thomas, is buried here, although I was unable to locate the slate headstone.

Next to the cemetery is a small but well-stocked antique shop owned by Ted Eayrs. The shop is open Saturdays from 9:00 A.M. to 5:00 P.M. When I visited with Ted, he showed me the ancient tractor he keeps in his barn—a 1937 McCormick Deering Farmall with steel wheels. Imagine how rough that ride must have been! Ted also keeps horses on his farm, and his home, barn, and fields are a perfect complement to the peacefulness of Titicut Green.

From the green it's a short drive or pleasant walk west on Plymouth Street to the banks of the Taunton River. Along the way you'll see a combination of fine old homes and rolling fields. On my last visit, during the late fall, a red-tailed hawk was perched in one of the large maple trees separating a field from the river. The bird looked as if it were asleep, but I have no doubt it had its eyes on the ground, looking for the movement of a mouse. If you look toward the back end of this field (on the left or south side of Plymouth Street), you will see a small hill in the distance. This is Fort Hill, once the site of a major Indian fort used by the local Wampanoags as protection against the mighty Narragansets who lived to the southwest.

The Taunton River was a major travel route for the Wampanoags, and the name Titicut is an Indian word meaning "place of the great river." A stone fish weir, located seventy-five feet above Pratt Bridge, is still visible in the river during periods of low water. Many of the roads we now travel were once Indian trails, and stone artifacts are still being found throughout southeastern Massachusetts when farmers plow their fields and gardeners turn the soil.

King Philip's War exploded in nearby Swansea, southwest of here, during the summer of 1675. Even within the

Titicut Parish Cemetery

confines of their fort, the settlers of Middleboro realized they might be overrun during those first days of bloodshed. In a letter to Governor Winslow dated July 10, Ensign Tomson asked for a guard to accompany the settlers out of the fort to the safety of Plymouth: "We are everyday liable to be a prey to our enemies, neither can we subsist here any longer by reason of want of provision and shot, for we are almost out of both." Imagine the fear within the tiny fort as the settlers watched more and more Indians arrive to burn the outlying homes.

One of the more interesting stories of the war is the tale of Mr. Richmond, an unusually large and powerful man, much hated and feared by the Indians because before the uprising, he had many victories over them in sporting contests. When hostilities began, Richmond became one of the scouts for the celebrated Indian fighter Benjamin Church, and immediately the Indians made him a top priority for capture or death. Toward the end of the war, the Indians were finally able to corner and kill him where Poquoy Brook enters the Taunton River. Years later when a highway was being repaired, Richmond's body was found and he was reinterred. His remains were later exhumed in the presence of doctors to examine his bones and see if his legendary size were true. After examination of the remains, it was estimated that his height was seven feet eight inches. The doctors also discovered that he had a double row of teeth in each jaw. No wonder the Indians were afraid!

It's a pleasure to stand on Pratt Bridge and watch the dark waters of the Taunton River roll by. "For the first time it occurred to me what a piece of wonder a river is," wrote Thoreau in his journal.

On the opposite side of the bridge is the town of Bridgewater. You might want to cross the river and go right on South Street to view an old millpond where a state-run foundry once made cannons. New England is loaded with the remains of old mills, many of which are now completely covered by the incursion of the woods. But if you walk around the perimeter of a stream-fed pond, there is a good chance you will see stone blocks or traces of a dike that once channeled the pond's water through a mill.

After you've enjoyed Titicut Green and the Taunton River, head east on Plymouth Street toward the center of Middleboro. Along the way, you will pass farm stands, old cemeteries, low-lying marshes, horse pastures, and some old Victorian homes. One of these homes (now a private residence) at the corner of Plymouth and Summer streets was once owned by the famous circus performers, General and Mrs. (Lavinia) Tom Thumb.

The great P.T. Barnum traveled to Middleboro in 1862 to meet the thirty-two-inch-tall Lavinia when she was twenty years old. A deal was struck, and Lavinia was paid an incredible one thousand dollars a week to appear at Barnum's American Museum in New York. It was there that she met Charles Stratton of Connecticut, better known as "General Tom Thumb of England." It wasn't long before they were married, pushing the news of the Civil War from the headlines of America's leading newspapers. The "Fairy Wedding" took place on February 10, 1863, and among the many famous guests were the President and Mrs. Lincoln.

After this tremendously successful and prosperous union, the couple built their home on Plymouth Street. Everything in it was built to their size: tiny furniture, kitchen cabinets placed low enough for them to reach, and even a miniature grand piano presented to them by Queen Victoria. Today, many of their possessions reside at the Middleboro Historical Museum. The grand piano, however, cannot be located. All that is known of its whereabouts is that it was first purchased from the estate in 1920 by an antique dealer who paid eleven dollars!

The historical museum, located on Jackson Street near the town's center, also features Indian artifacts, antique vehicles, a print shop, and an old-time country store with penny candy. It is open from 1:00 to 4:00 P.M. Wednesday through Sunday in July, August, and the first two weeks of September.

Just beyond the intersection of Plymouth Street and Route 44, you'll see a fascinating park on the right, begging for exploration. Over the years, the Oliver Mill picnic area was the site of a number of mills that used the water power of the Nemasket River. First, a gristmill ground corn—the major food of the settlers. Prior to the mill's construction in 1679, the settlers had to carry their corn all the way to Plymouth for grinding. Later, more mills were built, including a sawmill, an iron mill (producing cannon, mortar, howitzers, shot, and shells), a shovel factory, and a cider mill.

Reading *The History of the Town of Middleboro, Massachusetts*, I learned that "interesting archaeological research was carried out at the site of Judge Oliver's Iron Works when, in 1960, a project was launched to uncover the ruins of the forge and slitting mill. This program was accomplished chiefly through the enthusiasm of Fredrick Eayrs, Jr., then a high-school student who had become interested in archaeology." This is the same "Ted" Eayrs whom I met at the antique shop at Titicut Green; small world here in Middleboro.

Evidence of the mills can still be seen in the stonework found along the Nemasket River, where a number of foot bridges span channels of swift-flowing water. In the spring, the herring swim all the way from the ocean to this spot, and they have been harvested here for centuries. The herring was not only a major foodstuff of the Indians and settlers but also fertilizer for their corn. At one time, the fish were so thick that a basket could be dipped into the river and pulled up full of them. The herring run continues today (albeit with lesser numbers). When these small fish return each year to battle the river currents to complete their spawning mission, we can only marvel at nature.

The Oliver Mill picnic area is a pleasant place to stop for lunch or just to sit by the Nemasket River and listen to the soothing sound of the water. A number of picnic tables have views of the river, and kids can watch the ducks or maybe even spot a great blue heron.

Plymouth Street makes a left turn across from the Oliver Mill site and passes by the town's oldest cemetery, Nemasket Hill. Hilly lanes shaded by spruce trees make it an alluring place to explore. Farther down Plymouth Street, you will come to the intersection with Route 105. This crossroads is locally known as "the green," although there really isn't much of a green—at least not in the classic sense of Titicut Green. However, the green provides a good vantage point for seeing the massive First Congregational Church (1828) that sits far back on the left side of Route 105. Daniel Webster is said to have called it "the most beautiful church in New England." While I wouldn't go that far, it certainly is an imposing-looking building. At one time, this location was the center of Middleboro, and for years an area known as the "lower green" served as a military training ground.

Both east and west from this crossroads lie other interesting spots. Nature lovers: try going southwest a couple of minutes on Route 105 and stop at the 160-acre Pratt Farm Conservation Area. A number of enterprises once operated at what is now quiet meadows, marsh, and woods. There was a gristmill on Mill Pond, as well as an icehouse and cranberry bogs. In later years, dairy cows, beef cattle, and even a trout hatchery were located on the property. All that is gone now, but you can enjoy the relatively level hiking trails through peaceful acreage. In October a small fair is held here featuring music, country cooking, crafts, farm animals, nature exhibits, and events for the youngsters.

Traveling east on Plymouth Street, you will pass a small cranberry bog on your way to Carver, where even more bogs can be seen on the back roads or on Route 58. The Indians taught the Pilgrims how to use these crimson berries, and today a whole industry has evolved around them. Henry Hall of Cape Cod is said to have been the first person to realize the potential of cultivating the native plants when he noticed that those with sand blown around their bases grew the biggest berries. Cranberry bogs are now both natural and man-made marshes of rich soil or peat covered with a thin layer of sand. Harvesting has progressed from picking by hand to the current wet-harvesting method. Machinery (called waterwheels or eggbeaters) shake the berries from the vine, and then harvesters corral the floating berries and vacuum them through hoses into trucks.

The towns in southeastern Massachusetts, including Cape Cod, produce almost half the cranberry crop in the United States. (Ocean Spray Cranberry, Inc., an agricultural cooperative, is headquartered in nearby Lakeville.) The industry has been incredibly successful, diversifying from holiday side dishes to year-round products. New juices, such as cranberry and apple combinations, coupled with aggressive marketing, have produced impressive growth rates in consumer purchases.

A well-known attraction in the heart of cranberry country is Edaville Railroad, located on Route 58 in South Carver. Besides the five-and-a-half-mile train ride through the bogs and woodlands, Edaville has a petting zoo, a paddle-wheel steamboat, and a carousel. In an authentic version of a nineteenth-century shopping village, you can catch a trolley ride, climb aboard an old fire engine, or take the wheel of a Model T. In the crafts village, you'll view blacksmithing, basket weaving, woodworking, and quilt making performed by costumed interpreters. In the fall, enjoy the dazzling display of the cranberry harvest, and during the winter, the train runs through holiday displays illuminated by 200,000 Christmas lights. Some other special events include a Civil War Reenactment (second week of June), an Antique and Classic Auto Show (third Sunday in August), and the Custom Car Show (second Sunday in September).

Another interesting attraction in Carver is the King Richard's Faire, which features jousting, medieval music, food, and games. The Faire is held annually in the fall.

Cranberry Country: South to Buzzards Bay

South of Middleboro lie quiet villages and undiscovered, hidden coastal communities. Our exploration begins at Long Point Road, a causeway that runs along the northern edge of Great Quittacas Pond in the southwestern section of Middleboro. Great Quittacas Pond and Assawompsett Pond to the north are enormous bodies of fresh water, protected as reservoirs. This is one of the few places in eastern Massachusetts where the endangered bald eagle is sighted.

On a cold January morning, I drove slowly down Long Point Road, scanning the ice for any signs of movement. Three dark objects could be seen far out on the pond's frozen surface. Looking through my binoculars, I saw a large, mottled brown bird—probably an immature bald eagle. I then focused on the next object, and there was no question what this was. The white head and tail made the identification of the adult bald eagle unmistakable. The third object was unrecognizable—most likely the carrion that had attracted the eagles to this particular spot. Perhaps it was a dead white-tailed deer, run down on the ice by dogs or coyotes.

During the warmer weather months, the ponds are home to the osprey, another fish-eating raptor. Ospreys make their nests atop tall dead trees or specially erected poles next to a lake or the ocean. Like the eagle, the osprey population suffered from our use of the pesticide DDT. The deadly chemical worked its way through the food chain and caused alterations in the osprey's eggs, thus reducing the number of nestlings that survived. Restrictions on DDT have fostered a steady recovery in their numbers, but we may never again see full populations due to the increased development of coastal areas. It's a good thing that small portions of woodland or "accidental" wilderness were preserved as buffers surrounding our reservoirs.

Marion Road, a quiet, wooded country road, lies at the east end of Long Point Road. Follow this southward into Rochester, first going right on North Avenue, and then left on Snipatuit Road. The stone structure on the right side of Snipatuit Road was used as the town pound, where the early settlers placed runaway livestock. Remnants of stone pounds can be found all over New England, but few are as well preserved as this one.

After Snipatuit Road merges into Hartley Road, take a right onto Vaughn Hill Road. Cervelli Farm and Jonathan's Sprouts are located on the hill to the left. During the warm-weather months, the Cervelli Farm stand has sweet corn, strawberries, tomatoes, squash, peppers, lettuce, beans, peas, potatoes, and other popular New England vegetables. In the fall, you can purchase pumpkins and Indian corn, and in the winter, you can choose and cut your own Christmas tree.

It is becoming increasingly hard to find farms like this in eastern Massachusetts because escalating land values make development much more profitable than farming. Sadly, New Englanders are becoming more and more dependent on sunbelt- and foreign-grown produce. The remaining family-run farms need all the business we can give them. Besides the obvious advantage of giving us fresh produce, the farmlands help give our country roads the feeling of openness and solitude that we cherish.

Located inside the large barn at Cervelli Farm is Jonathan's Sprouts, New Englands pioneer sprout company.

They offer tours to the public by appointment. Unlike other crops, the sprouts grow entirely free of soil, needing only moisture to reach the harvesting stage. Sprouting increases the nutritional value of seeds; they retain the original B-complex, and in the process of sprouting they dramatically increase vitamins A and C. Best of all, they require no pesticides.

On my tour, manager Bea Escalante first showed me the growing room, where the mung beans are cultivated inside the total darkness of stainless steel cylinders. The walls of the room were dripping wet to help keep the humidity at high levels for peak growing. The juicy sprouts have a subtle, nutty flavor and are good sources of protein. Alfalfa sprouts are grown out in the open in an adjoining room, where both light and water are highly regulated; rigid time schedules must be followed to produce a superior product. Both types of sprouts require a labor-intensive process combining hard work with a tender touch.

From Vaughn Hill Road, it's just a short drive to the Mattapoisett waterfront, situated on Buzzards Bay. This quaint little town has yet to be discovered by the throngs of tourists who invade Cape Cod.

On the ocean side of Water Street, across from the old Mattapoisett Inn, is a picturesque patch of greenery called Shipyard Park. You can sit in the park's bandstand, with its whale weather vane, and watch the harbor activity while the smells of the sea are carried ashore by the ocean breeze. Each July, a Harbor Day festival—complete with food, crafts, and music—is held in the park.

Shipyard Park commemorates the Mattapoisett shipbuilders, who were active from 1752 to 1878. Brigs, schooners, sloops, and merchant ships were all built here, including the Platina, distinguished for capturing a white whale. The stone memorial at Shipyard Park says that in 1840 Herman Melville was a crew member on the locally built *Acushnet* during her maiden voyage. The Mattapoisett Historical Society and Carriage House, located on Church Street, has exhibits from those early seafaring days.

The charming Mattapoisett Inn, built in 1790, is advertised as the oldest seaside inn in the nation still *operating* as an inn in its original structure. Originally, the building was a general store and tavern where men from the shipyard gathered at " 'leven an' four" each day for a rum break. Today, the inn's claim to fame is its excellent food, served in an authentic old-New England setting, and in the warm weather, you can dine out on the front porch. Upstairs there is lodging in three antique-filled rooms with ocean views. If you yearn for a quiet stay, however, be warned that live entertainment can reverberate throughout the inn on Thursday, Friday, and Saturday evenings.

For those who delight in taking solitary walks along rocky coastlines, Ned's Point lies just to the east of Shipyard Park on Mattapoisett Harbor. It's a romantic little knob of land, dominated by a small lighthouse that was erected in 1888. I stopped here during the off-season and sat on a boulder munching a sandwich (which included sprouts fresh from Jonathan's). An assortment of sea ducks, some with vivid black and white coloring, bobbed in the waves just a few feet in front of me. I would have sat there for hours if not for a chilling breeze, but I vowed to come back in April with my wife.

From Ned's Point, you can drive east on Route 6 into Marion, or better yet, with the aid of a detailed map, take the back roads and discover the many coves and points of land that grace this shoreline. Marion is a charming old village on the bay that has antique shops, bookstores, and an old general store; great for browsing. Both Main and Front streets are lined with handsome homes and cottages.

To complete our loop, we take Route 105 all the way back to Middleboro. Normally any road with a route number has traffic—but not this one. Commercial development has not yet spoiled the southern part of this road, and you can still enjoy the freedom of traveling at slow speeds through quiet country towns. The center of Rochester is a perfect example. I had never even heard of the town until my trip to Buzzards Bay, and was pleasantly surprised when I stumbled upon the scenic old town hall and First Congregational Church that bracket the town common. Even the minimall across the street is tastefully done, at least attempting to be unobtrusive to the character of the place. Across from an old graveyard, you'll find a smaller green where an old signpost, showing the mileage to all the nearby towns, stands next to an ancient hand pump.

Another spot that caught my eye on Route 105 was a simple building set behind an old stone wall near the town line of Lakeville and Acushnet. It was the Long Plain Friends Meetinghouse, circa 1755. Listed in the National Register of Historic Places, this unadorned Quaker meetinghouse was used for gatherings of worship without fixed religious rituals. The Quakers originally called themselves Friends, and the word Quaker was originally one of ridicule, coined in 1650 by an English magistrate who used it sarcastically because the Friends "tremble at the word of the Lord." Their first stronghold in colonial America was in Rhode Island, known for its religious tolerance.

The stone wall in front of the meetinghouse is worth a long look. Massive blocks fit almost perfectly, allowing little light to filter through, and smaller stones have been inserted in the occasional open crevice. Notice how level the top of the wall is—a real feat, considering the different sizes of the rocks and the annual havoc that frost can cause. One can only imagine the labor and time that must have gone into building such a wall, at a time when farmers had the aid of only oxen or horses.

The final few miles back to Middleboro and Route 495 are pleasant ones, passing by orchards and along the edge of Little Quittacas Pond, Great Quittacas Pond, and Assawompsett Pond. Route 105 will eventually lead to Route 18, at the northern end of Assawompsett Pond, and this can be followed back to the starting point, where we first visited Titicut Green.

In the Area

All numbers are within area code 508.

Middleboro Chamber of Commerce: 947-1499
Edaville Railroad (South Carver): 866-4526
Middleboro Historical Museum: 947-1969
Jonathan's Sprouts (Rochester): 763-2577
Mattapoisett Historical Society and Carriage House: 758-2844
Hell's Blazes Restaurant (Middleboro): 295-9111
King Richard's Faire (Carver town hall): 866-3403
Days Inn (Middleboro): 946-4400
Suisse Chalet (Middleboro): 1-800-258-1980
KOA Campground (Middleboro): 947-6435
Mattapoisett Inn: 758-4922

9 ~ The South Shore

Take exit 14 off Route 3 and go north on Route 228 about six miles to where it intersects Route 3A. Go left on 3A to Hingham and World's End Reservation. This trip explores the shore just south of Boston from Hingham to Duxbury.

Highlights: *World's End Reservation, herons, hawks, egrets and swans, South Shore Arts Festival in the summer, Maritime Museum, rhododendrons at Whitney Thayer Reservation, Stockbridge cemetery, sundews and pitcher plants at Black Pond Reservation, the North River, Daniel Webster's farm, Winslow House, bluefishing, Duxbury Beach, Myles Standish's homesite.*

Without following the throngs of tourists to Plymouth, you can find much to see on the South Shore below Boston. In fact, the most pleasant roads bypass the Plymouth waterfront entirely to wander a countryside equally rich in history and wildlife. For example, you can visit Duxbury, where Myles Standish lived, or Marshfield, where the North River flows, once the scene of numerous shipyards. Today the shipyards are gone, but you can view their locations and walk in solitude along this incredibly scenic tidal river. On weekdays between 9:00 A.M. and 3:00 P.M. and on weekends, especially

Sunday morning, the traffic is light—a good time to explore these Boston suburbs.

The wildlife—especially the migratory birds that stop along the South Shore—is as fascinating as the history. For diversity of wildlife coupled with splendid views, the World's End Reservation in Hingham is hard to top. When you get to Hingham, follow the signs around the rotary directing you to Nantasket on Summer Street. Follow this for four-tenths of a mile and then turn left on Martin Lane. World's End is at the end of this street. The admission fee is modest and well worth it. Occasionally the parking lot fills up on spring weekends. Allow yourself a couple of hours to spend at World's End.

The views here are spectacular—to the west and northwest you can see the Boston skyline and some of the Harbor Islands, while Nantasket lies to the northeast and east. Glaciers formed the two smooth, elongated hills or drumlins at World's End. These drumlins are now primarily open land covered in fields and meadows. In 1890, famed landscape architect Frederick Law Olmstead designed the paths and plantings found throughout the reservation for a development that fortunately was never completed. Today The Trustees of Reservations own the land and keep it open for all to enjoy.

The bird life here is incredible: black capped night herons, harrier hawks, cormorants, great blue herons, snowy egrets, quails, kestrels, and, of course, wide-ranging red-tailed hawks. Ask Ranger Mahoney to show you the beautiful mute swan with its pure white coloring and long, graceful neck in the marsh pond just beyond the ranger station.

To make pasture land, early colonists stripped World's End almost entirely of its timber. Olmstead planted many of the trees you see, including the imported English oaks that line the paths. Settlers built a causeway linking Planters Hill, the first drumlin, with World's End drumlin. At one time

The South Shore

Cohasset town green

Boston itself was like this: a hilly peninsula linked to the mainland only by a soggy, narrow neck.

Don't overlook Rocky Neck, a point of land situated on a rocky cliff. Unlike the two open drumlins, Rocky Neck is wooded. A hiker walks through cool, shaded trails to the cliff's edge above the rocky shore. In 1909, farmers built an ice pond nearby. Today the little pond is an enchanting place to sit and quietly observe the birds and animals that frequent it. Look for cottontails or red foxes along the pond's edge or on the nearby trail.

I once saw a red fox here—one of the handsomest animals I have ever seen. It bounded gracefully through the woods, stopping occasionally to look back at me. You can sometimes see foxes hunting for mice in the open fields, but I'm sure this one was after a more substantial meal of rabbit from Rocky Neck.

Continue your South Shore trip by following Martin Lane back to Summer Street and swing left. It's easy to get lost on these back roads but that's fine—just stay near the shore for the best views. (You can always find your way back to Route

3A.) Proceed down Summer Street to Rockland Street, then to Jerusalem Road. A number of coves, tidal marshes and rocky ocean vistas greet you on your way. I once watched a great blue heron, bathed in early morning sunlight, hunt along a small salt marsh next to Jerusalem Road. The bird would pause, take a careful step, then pause again as it searched for small fish to snatch with its long bill. World's End is not the only place to look for migratory birds—they can be seen all along the South Shore wherever you find open space and water.

Follow Jerusalem Road, where the homes and mansions are known locally as "millionaire's row," to Atlantic Avenue. Take Elm Street into quaint Cohasset, where the First Parish Church (1747) shares the town common with a duck pond. Visit Saint Stephen's Church with its fifty-seven-bell carillon, the largest in New England. Concerts are given from late June through August on Sundays at 6:00 P.M. Art lovers should visit the South Shore Art Center on nearby Riply Road, where they exhibit the work of Massachusetts artists and host an art festival each summer on the common—the longest running art festival in the country.

History buffs will enjoy the Maritime Museum on Elm Street. It includes photographs, carvings, equipment, and models of the shipping trade that once thrived here, as well as Indian artifacts and other historic items.

Thoreau visited Cohasset on his way to Cape Cod in October 1849. He wrote about the violent storm that struck the coast and the handbill that shouted, "Death! one hundred and forty-five lives lost at Cohasset." The *St. John*, a ship loaded with immigrants from Ireland, had wrecked off this rocky coast just three days prior to his visit, and Thoreau reported: "Many horses in carriages were fastened to the fences near the shore, and, for a mile or more, up and down, the beach was covered with people looking out for bodies and examining the fragments of the wreck. . . . In the very midst of the crowd about this wreck, there were men with carts busily collecting the seaweed which the storm had cast up, and conveying it beyond the reach of the tide, though they were often obliged to separate fragments of clothing from it, and they might at any moment have found a human body under it. Drown who might, they did not forget that this weed was a valuable manure. This shipwreck had not produced a visible vibration in the fabric of society." The complete account of Thoreau's journey can be found in his book *Cape Cod*.

    Drive to the end of the town green and go left on Sohier Road all the way to Route 3A. At this intersection you may want to stop to explore Whitney Thayer Reservation, located just on the other side of Route 3A, especially beautiful in the spring when rhododendrons bloom along the Milliken Trail. Proceed south on Route 3A into Scituate, and then go right on Booth Hill Road or Mann Lot Road, then right again on Thomas Clapp Road. These quiet, wooded residential streets lead into Norwell, perhaps my favorite South Shore town because of all its open space and conservation land.

    Thomas Clapp Road leads into Mount Blue Street. Drive a short way left down Mount Blue Street. On the left, the tiny Stockbridge Cemetery perches on a small hill next to the road. It's a quiet spot, one of those forgotten places that make New England back roads so special. One headstone caught my attention: Mr. James Stockbridge who died at age 80 in 1819. His inscription reads

> You turnest man, O Lord to dust
> Of which he first was made;
> And when thou speakest the word return,
> Tis instantly obey'd.

    From the cemetery continue down Mount Blue Street for eight-tenths of a mile to visit Black Pond Nature Preserve.

Telephone the Massachusetts Audubon Society for permission to enter, which is required because of the fragile nature of this kettle-hole sphagnum bog surrounded by an Atlantic white cedar swamp. The Audubon Society manages the property for the Nature Conservancy, which owns many ecologically sensitive and unique reservations in the state.

Carnivorous sundews and pitcher plants, which trap and digest insects, grow in the sanctuary. You can reach the quaking cedar bog in a fifteen-minute walk. On the way, you pass through a grove of hemlock, beech, and American holly trees before reaching the boardwalk through the swampy area surrounded by American cedars. Large ferns and other vegetation give you the sense of being in a jungle.

Settlers once prized these cedars for lumber because the wood resisted decay, making it perfect for fence posts, wooden shingles, piers, gutters, and boat-building material. Because of the extensive logging done in the past, the trees growing here now are quite rare.

A mat of floating sphagnum moss rings the small pond. Recognizing the absorbent features of the moss, Native Americans used the material to line their babies' diapers. Don't expect to see much wildlife at the edge of the pond—only a limited variety of aquatic life can grow in the relatively sterile waters of the bog, which is low in oxygen and nutrients. I do a lot of walking in Massachusetts reservations and sanctuaries and I find this to be one of the most interesting of all.

From Black Pond, drive on to the North River. The North River gives the South Shore its identity: it's rich with history, scenery, and wildlife. Perhaps the best way to explore the river other than by canoe is to visit the Norris Reservation. Continue down Mount Blue Street, take a right on Old Oaken Bucket Road, and then a left on Central Street. This takes you to tiny Norwell center where you cross Route 123; then take a left on West Street to the reservation's parking lot.

A wide, well-groomed trail leads from the parking area to a small millpond where a gristmill and sawmill operated in 1690. Just beyond the pond, American holly trees grow beneath pine, oak, maple, and beech. The holly, a deciduous evergreen, cannot survive in extremely cold temperatures. The trees in this vicinity mark their northernmost limit.

About twenty minutes further down the trail, you will see the waters of the North River. This is an estuarine waterway where the tidal flows from the ocean mix salt water with the river's own fresh water. Because of this unique mixture, only certain kinds of vegetation can thrive here. Salt hay spans broadly over the muddy shoreline. When you walk down to the river, bring your camera to capture the vivid colors of a sunny day. The greens and golds of the salt marsh contrast with the ribbon of blue winding through its heart. A telephoto lens might also come in handy; you never know when a harrier hawk will hover above the marsh.

Just a short distance east of Norwell center and the Norris Reservation is the Bridge Street–Union Street Bridge over the North River. Bridge Street is on the right-hand side of Route 123; after passing over the river into Marshfield, it becomes Union Street. Settled in 1632, Marshfield got its name for the many marshes scattered about, most of which were drained in earlier times to raise cranberries or strawberries. Besides viewing the river from the bridge, you can stretch your legs and get a closer look at the water by taking a quick right just after the bridge to a small parking lot owned by the Marshfield Conservation Commission.

Continuing down Union Street, take a right on Cornhill Lane. Rogers Shipyards operated at the end of Cornhill Lane from 1790 to 1820 and produced over twenty-three vessels between 20 and 221 tons. A large cast-iron sign from 1919 marks the exact location of the shipyard. Master shipwrights built over a thousand ships along the North River, including the *Beaver* of Boston Tea Party fame. Teams of oxen dragged to the yards white pine for masts and white oak for hulls. When the surrounding timber was cut, and the size of the vessels became too large to float down the river, the shipyards closed.

People who explore the river by canoe or boat should remember it is a tidal river requiring extra care. The area downstream from the Union Street Bridge—getting closer to the ocean—becomes increasingly more dangerous as the tides exert more pressure on the river. Where the river meets the ocean is especially dangerous, and many a careless boater has lost his life there. Small vessels should avoid this area entirely.

From Cornhill Lane, go back up Union Street and take a right on Highland Street. It's a lovely area of colonial homes, fields, and fieldstone walls. Rogers Pond lies at the intersection of Highland and Spring streets, once the site of many different enterprises such as a gristmill, a tannery, and a rivet factory.

Follow Highland Street east to Route 3A, go right (south), then left on Route 139, and right onto Daniel Webster Street, and finally left on Winslow Cemetery Road, where the famous statesman is buried in Winslow Cemetery. For twenty years Webster lived in Marshfield on this street. His farm was huge, growing a wide variety of vegetables fertilized with kelp and menhaden, an oily ocean fish. He also kept cattle, sheep, swine, poultry, and horses. It is said he respected horses so much that he buried them with halters and shoes on, in an upright position. In 1979, this tale was proved true when excavations uncovered the bones of three horses, all buried upright.

Webster once said, "It is wise for us to recur to the history of our ancestors. Those who do not look upon themselves as a link connecting the Past with the Future do not perform their duty to the World." Upon Webster's death in 1852, Ralph

Waldo Emerson remarked, "America and the world has lost the completest man." One of his remarkable achievements was that he served as secretary of state under three different presidents, a feat that would be next to impossible in modern times.

At the end of Winslow Cemetery Road lie the open fields and marshes of Daniel Webster Wildlife Sanctuary. It's only a short walk to the top of Fox Hill overlooking the quiet meadows. From this vantage point you can see a pole with a large nest on top rising from the wetlands. This is an osprey nest. With a pair of binoculars you might be able to spot this magnificent bird. This is the first successful osprey nest found anywhere along the South Shore in over a hundred years. You can identify the bird by its distinctive brown and white markings and five-foot wingspan with a conspicuous crook in the middle of each wing. If I could be any bird, I'd be an osprey; they spend their entire day fishing!

Where Webster Street intersects with Careswell Street (Route 139), you can see the original Winslow School, a one-room schoolhouse built in 1857. On the right is the Winslow House built in 1699, said to be in the most original condition of any of the old homes of the descendants of the Pilgrims. The Winslow family came to America on the *Mayflower*; Edward Winslow was the first person to settle in Marshfield. As one of the leaders of Plymouth Colony, Winslow constructed the 1622 agreement between the Pilgrims and Massasoit, the leader of the Wampanoag Indian tribe. The agreement lasted some fifty-three years until the outbreak of war led by another Wampanoag leader, Metacom or "Philip," who ironically was the son of Massasoit.

Don't miss a special feature of the Winslow House—the Jacobean stairway with heavy balusters, newel posts, and acorn drops. You can take a tour from mid-June through mid-October, Wednesday through Sunday from 1:00 P.M. to 5:00 P.M. Also on the grounds are Daniel Webster's law office and a carriage house containing the Concord coach, which once carried passengers and mail from Marshfield to Hingham to meet the packet ship to Boston.

After touring the Winslow House, go right on Route 139 and travel south on Route 3A into Duxbury. You can reach the quiet coastal areas near Duxbury Bay by St. George Street and Powder Point Avenue. At the end of Powder Point Avenue is the Powder Point Bridge, the longest wooden bridge on the eastern seaboard. Whoever constructed this bridge did it right: a wide walkway lets pedestrians enjoy a view of the bay or watch sailboarders whiz by. Although you can drive over this 2,200-foot-long bridge, walking lets you gab with the fishermen who angle there for flounder, bluefish, and striped bass.

I've had the pleasure of some fine bluefishing from the bridge; it's always a challenge to bring the fish from the water all the way up to the top of the bridge. Local anglers lower a giant treble hook on a rope to act as a gaff and then haul up the fish. One September morning I snagged a pogie (also known as menhaden), and a large blue or striper grabbed the bait. For a good thirty seconds the brute stripped line off my reel as my drag made noises I'd never heard before. It took a while, but I finally applied enough pressure to slow the fish down. I was already thinking of hollering to a fellow angler to come over with a rope gaff, or perhaps of walking the fish down to the end of the bridge where I could beach it. But my plans were premature because my line snapped—or so I thought. When I reeled in the line, I discovered it had not been severed, but one of the hooks on my treble hook, which was used to snag the pogie, was bent so much it was embedded in the lead shaft. Whatever species of fish I had been battling—probably a large bluefish—must have had incredibly strong jaws to do that.

The South Shore

On the other side of Powder Point Bridge is Duxbury Beach, a nine-mile barrier beach open to the general public. I enjoy the beach in the off-season, when you can take long, solitary walks by the open sea. The "no-name storm" of 1991 shifted the beach sands and rocks considerably, but the same sands helped to protect the homes across the bay. The more exposed coastal sections, especially those along Marshfield's Brant Rock section, were not as lucky. One relative of mine lost his entire home to that surprise autumn storm.

From the Powder Point Bridge, follow King Caesar's Road away from the bridge to a small half-acre park on the waterfront. A stone seat overlooking the Bay makes this a perfect spot to soak up the sights, smells, and sounds of the ocean. Nearby is the King Caesar House, a Federal-style mansion built in 1808 by Ezra Weston II, which is open for tours during warm-weather months. Don't miss the period furnishings and rare French mural wallpapers. Weston and his father, two wealthy, powerful men who made their money as merchants and shipbuilders, shared the nickname "King Caesar."

Take a short ride south on Washington Street to South Duxbury, our final destination. Turn onto Standish Street to reach the knob of land jutting into Duxbury Bay that was once the home of the military leader of Plymouth Colony, Myles Standish. At Standish Reservation a huge stone tower stands with a statue of old Myles himself on top. Cars are not allowed up the access road from Labor Day to Memorial Day, but it's a short walk to the monument. Standish, in my opinion, was not exactly a hero to be exalted. An effective protector from the Pilgrims' perspective, his sometimes harsh treatment of the Indians did little to encourage cooperation between the two cultures. However, it's hard to pass judgment on people whose very survival was an uncertainty. There are a number of good books on the early settlement of the Plymouth area, and one of my favorites is *The English to New England* by Douglas Hill.

While the Standish Monument is worth visiting, I prefer the Standish homesite, located at the end of Mayflower Road. Whatever your feelings about Standish, you must agree he knew his real estate: the coastal view from the back of his homesite is spectacular. Steps lead down from the little park to the shore below, another good spot to enjoy the ocean.

Drive south from Duxbury to reach the historic Plymouth waterfront. Plymouth is too crowded for my taste, but you may want to explore Old Sandwich Road, which leads toward Cape Cod.

In the Area

All numbers are within area code 617.

Hingham Chamber of Commerce: 749-4806

Cohasset Chamber of Commerce: 383-1010

Marshfield-Scituate Chamber of Commerce: 834-0134

Massachusetts Audubon Society, South Shore: 837-9400

Saint Stephen's Church: carillon concert (Cohasset): 383-1083

South Shore Art Center (Cohasset): 383-9548

Cohasset Maritime Museum: 383-6930

Winslow House (Marshfield):837-5753

King Caesar House (Duxbury): 934-6106

Myles Standish Monument (South Duxbury): 866-2526

Duxbury Beach: 837-3112

Gurnet Inn (Marshfield): 834-7141

Winsor House Inn (Duxbury): 934-0991

Kimballs Motor Inn (Cohasset): 383-6650

The South Shore

Red Lion Inn (Cohasset): 383-1704

Milepost Tavern Restaurant (Duxbury): 934-6801

Bittersweet Farm: pick-your-own flowers (Duxbury): 934-2788

Tree-Berry Farm: pick-your-own blueberries and choose-and-cut Christmas trees (Scituate): 834-7514

Marshfield Fair: August; call the town hall at 834-5540 or chamber of commerce at 834-0134

10 ~ Overlooked Mashpee: Cape Cod

Take Route 28 south on Cape Cod to Route 151. Follow 151 to where it crosses Route 28 again at the Mashpee Rotary. This trip explores the southwest shore of Cape Cod between Mashpee and East Falmouth.

Highlights: *Holly and Franklinia trees at Ashumet Holly Reservation, Mashpee Wampanoag Indian Museum and annual powwow; fishing in both fresh and salt water, picnicking at Lowell Holly Reservation; Cahoon Museum of American Art, Barnstable County Fair, South Cape Beach, shoreline drives, Mashpee River Reservation.*

Snow so white it hurt the eyes. A steel blue sky above. And stretching to the horizon, the gray-blue waters of Nantucket Sound. Farther down the shore, patches of gold showed where the wind had swept the snow from the tops of exposed dunes. Tracks were scattered about. White-tailed deer had been here at night.

Winter on Cape Cod. The Cape has a reserved beauty during the winter, difficult to find during the crowded summer months. Now is the time to walk the beach or explore the inland woods. The flocks of tourists who jam the canal bridges each weekend from Memorial Day through Labor Day are gone. Few visitors come during the spring and fall, and hardly anyone comes in the winter. Each season has its special features, and although this outing is primarily geared toward winter, we cover a number of warmer weather activities as well.

Choosing an area of the Cape to explore is difficult indeed. I've always been partial to Wellfleet, Orleans, and Mashpee. Mashpee is often bypassed by visitors who cross the canal heading for the more well-known Dennis, Hyannis, and Yarmouth. But it would be a mistake to miss the back roads of Mashpee, Cotuit, East Falmouth, and North Falmouth, with their many wildlife reservations, quiet shorelines, museums, and antique shops. Another factor which makes the area so special is the rich Native American presence; Mashpee is still home to over 600 Wampanoag Indians.

The focal point of this Upper Cape excursion is the Mashpee rotary, where Route 151 meets Route 28. From here, you can branch out in any direction and see some of the Cape's natural beauty. (Thoreau enjoyed the Cape so much he visited four times: in 1849, 1850, 1855, and 1857.)

Most visitors to Mashpee will be coming west on Route 151 toward the Mashpee rotary. On the left side of the road, in East Falmouth, you will see the Massachusetts Audubon Society's distinctive blue and white sign pointing the way to the forty-five-acre Ashumet Holly Reservation and Wildlife Sanctuary. The sanctuary is known for its sixty-five varieties of holly trees, many of which were propagated by Wilfrid Wheeler, the state's first commissioner of agriculture. In 1925, Wheeler began selecting the best specimen native hollies, saying that he wished to "perpetuate them against destruction not only from people but from fires and increasing construction work."

A path circles the reservation, passing through fields, around the shore of Grassy Pond, and through a magnificent stand of hollies with their dark, shiny, green leaves. The property also features unusual Franklinia trees that flower in the fall. Mixed among the hollies and Franklinia trees are the sandy-soil-loving scrub oak, red cedar, and pitch pine—the three most common trees on the Cape.

Roughly 133 species of birds have been spotted here, including downy woodpeckers, ruffed grouse, northern orioles, ring-necked pheasants, and an enormous colony of barn swallows which inhabit the barn during the warmer months. The sanctuary hosts special events such as Holly Days in early December, an open house in the spring, and the Franklinia Festival in the fall. Call the Ashumet Holly Reservation for information.

Imagine how beautiful the Cape must have been when it was left in its natural state and the only inhabitants were the original owners, the Native Americans. You can relive those days by visiting the Mashpee Wampanoag Indian Museum on Route 130. Take Central Road northward from the rotary, then go left a few feet on Route 130.

This small museum, housed in an old Cape Cod half-house built in 1793, rarely gets crowded, and the exhibits would be of interest to children as well as adults. The museum displays the history and culture of the Wampanoag Indians from the Stone Age to the present. You will see Indian heirlooms, tools, baskets, hunting and fishing implements, weapons, and domestic utensils. A large mural depicts a lakeside scene from an early Wampanoag settlement. It shows the Indian's unique way of bringing down a tree by building a fire at the base of its trunk. A clay barrier was placed a few feet above the fire, surrounding the trunk, to stop the fire from spreading up the entire tree. The museum is open year-round, Tuesday through Saturday, from 10:00 A.M. to 2:00 P.M. If you visit in the spring, be sure to walk to the edge of the museum's parking lot to see the tiny, clear-flowing Mashpee River where the herring make their annual run.

Overlooked Mashpee: Cape Cod

On one of my visits to Mashpee, I had the good fortune to meet a Wampanoag woman who shared her views with me. I asked her what she thought of the recent surge of interest in Native Americans, and she responded, "The appreciation of our culture is most welcome; however, it is probably a little too late. So much of our way of life has been altered, and the earth continues to be spoiled. I feel bad for our children; they are missing so much. Even the wild creatures have nowhere to go. We are changing too much of the land. We need to protect what's left. No matter what your beliefs, we are all children of the Great Creator, and we must save the land."

The Wampanoag Indians still hold a large, three-day powwow in Mashpee, every July Fourth weekend. Indians from all over the United States are invited to the celebration, and the public is invited to enjoy the food, crafts, exhibits, and dancing. Call the Wampanoag Tribal Council for more information.

Just a couple of minutes from the museum lies The Old Indian Meetinghouse, located on Meetinghouse Road. Established in 1637 by missionary John Eliot, this was the first Indian church in the United States. The original building was moved in 1717 from Bryants Neck to the current location, and was completely restored in 1969. On special occasions, worship services are still conducted in the Algonquian Indian language by Wampanoag preachers. The old cemetery adjacent to the meetinghouse has been used by the Mashpee Wampanoags since before the *Mayflower*.

One of the largest Indian settlements was located on the shore of Mashpee and Wakeby ponds. These two ponds are linked by a narrow channel to form the largest body of fresh water on the Cape. Deep and clear, the ponds are among the loveliest found anywhere, and they offer excellent angling for trout, largemouth bass, and feisty smallmouth bass. In fact, the hundreds of Cape Cod "kettle-hole" ponds—deep, spring-fed ponds formed by glaciers—offer some of the best fishing in New England. Smallmouth bass (or "bronzeback") fishing is especially good. Unlike their largemouth cousins, the smallmouths can only survive in lakes that are deep enough to remain cool even in the dog days of summer, and the kettle-hole ponds are perfect habitat for these terrific fighters. Trout also benefit from the deep water, and during the springtime you don't need a boat to catch them; just cast your lure, fly, or bait from shore.

Of course, Cape Cod is best known for its tremendous saltwater fishing. You can charter a boat for a group of four to six people and angle for such species as bluefish or striped bass, both of which give you a battle you won't forget. Party boats are also available, seeking bottom fish such as the cod for which the Cape is named. Nearby Falmouth has a fleet of fishing boats accommodating the public in the warm-weather months. Call the Falmouth Chamber of Commerce for more information.

Another good summertime activity is to view the sparkling waters of Mashpee–Wakeby Ponds from the wooded shores of Lowell Holly Reservation, located off South Sandwich Road in Mashpee. (The reservation is open daily from May 30 to October 1 from 10:00 A.M. to 5:00 P.M. Admission is charged on weekends and holidays. Visitors are welcome to sunbathe and swim off the sandy beach; picnic tables are positioned for scenic views of the water as well as cooling lakeside breezes.)

Lowell Holly Reservation is the peninsula that separates Mashpee Pond from Wakeby Pond, and is best known for its impressive stand of enormous beech trees. The beautiful, smooth gray trunks of the beeches contrast nicely with the handsome green leaves of the holly trees that grow in the understory of the taller hardwoods. Except for the cart paths constructed by the former owner, Dr. Abbott Lowell, the reservation has been left pretty much in its natural state for the last 200 years. Trails lead through the peninsula all the way to its tip, where you can sit by the channel that connects the two ponds and feel as if you're on an island.

Peters Pond, in nearby Sandwich, is another clean, spring-fed pond with great fishing and boating. Peters Pond Campground offers some great waterside camping, as well as boat rentals. It is a popular spot, so be sure to call first.

South on Route 130, at its intersection with Route 28 in Cotuit, is an area where you can find antique shops, a gift shop, and the Cahoon Museum of American Art. The museum is housed in a red and white Cape Cod colonial built in 1775. Ezra Crocker and his wife Temperance once ran a tavern in the building. Visitors such as Daniel Webster would stop to rest there during a trip on the Hyannis–Sandwich stagecoach line. Today, the building houses the work of a variety of artists including William Matthew Prior, Alvan Fisher, James E. Butterworth, Dwight W. Tryon, John J. Enneking, and Ralph and Mary Cahoon. The collection spans pre-Revolutionary times to the present; marine and ocean paintings are especially well represented. The museum is

The Falmouth shore on Cape Cod

open Wednesday through Saturday from 10:00 A.M. to 4:00 P.M., and on Sundays from 1:00 to 4:00 P.M.

Quiet Cotuit center lies a couple of miles down Main Street from the Cahoon Museum. This oceanside town, which has protected itself from commercialism and development, is worth a visit. Narrow Main Street passes by stately clapboarded houses, the weather-shingled town library, Cotuit Freedom Hall (1860), and the Old Meetinghouse (1846).

Leaving Cotuit, go west on School Street, which leads to Quinaquisset Street, past the scenic inlet at Popponessett Bay which is fed by the Quaker, Santuit, and Mashpee rivers. Look for an assortment of ducks and gulls bobbing in the bay, and herons stalking the shoreline.

Quinaquisset Road brings you back to Route 28, where 375-acre Mashpee River Reservation protects this important watershed. On the south side of Route 28 you'll see a dirt-road entrance to the reservation with limited parking; additional parking can be found across the street on Meetinghouse Road. You can hike along a scenic riverside trail that follows the river downstream through the woodlands. The reservation is owned by The Trustees of Reservations, one of the foremost conservation organizations in the state. They have bought and protected many unique and ecologically sensitive natural areas, saving them from development, and allowing public access for free or for a small admission charge.

The Mashpee River flows southward into a saltwater estuary, and although it's a small, relatively shallow river, it supports a population of unique sea-run brown trout. The Massachusetts Division of Fisheries and Wildlife has labored long and hard to develop this strain of anadromous brown trout, keyed to Cape Cod streams. Trout Unlimited has assisted in the effort by restoring sections of Cape streams by clearing brush sections and installing overhead cover. The efforts have been successful, but catching these elusive creatures is another matter: only the most patient, crafty anglers have a shot at a hookup. I've heard of beginner's luck, but I've yet to see it occur when it comes to river angling for brown trout!

From Mashpee River Reservation it's just a hop southwestward on Route 28 to return to the Mashpee rotary. The Barnstable County fairgrounds are located near here, about a half-mile west of the rotary, on Route 151. An annual event, the Barnstable County Fair is usually held in late July, and is one of the oldest county/agricultural fairs in Massachusetts. It features exhibition square dancing, crafts, livestock, and horse-pulling contests.

Directly to the south of the Mashpee circle is South Cape Beach, situated at the end of Great Neck Road and Oak Road. Whenever I wander along a secluded beach in winter, I think of Henry Beston, the author of the beloved classic *The Outermost House*, his story about a year he spent alone living in a small house on a Cape Cod beach. Beston described a winter walk on the beach as follows: "As I walk the beach on a bright and blustery January morning, my first impression is one of space, beauty, and loneliness." He describes the snow on the beach grass as having "the quality and delicacy of Japanese painting." For anyone who loves the Cape, this book about the natural world of ocean and shore is one to read over and over.

South Cape Beach has excellent wildlife viewing for shore birds and raptors; ospreys have nested in the nearby marsh, and visitors can sometimes see them wing over the water as they hunt for fish. Besides viewing nature from the beach, a hiking trail just off the access road leads to Great Flat Pond.

Red Brook Road is a pleasant side street that leads from Great Neck Road to Route 28, where we head south into Falmouth. Then look for Central Avenue on the left, which leads down to Manauhant Road following the shoreline of Nantucket Sound. I once saw two pure white mute swans winging their way along the coast parallel to the road, and then minutes later enjoyed watching a harrier hawk hover above a marshy cove. Manauhant Road leads into Ocean Avenue followed by Grand Avenue, which climbs the small oceanside cliffs at Falmouth Heights.

If you wish to explore Falmouth center, continue westward on Grand Avenue, but be warned that this lovely town gets its share of traffic. The inland regions of Falmouth, however, are less congested, and you can even find a handful of farms. Try following Carriage Shop Road, which passes a small cranberry bog, to Old Meetinghouse Road on the left. This is where you will find the Tony Andrews Farm. Tony Andrews had trouble finding labor to work his fields after World War II, and in 1954 he decided to alleviate the problem by introducing the "pick-your-own" concept, probably the first in the state. You can wander the fields picking your own strawberries, peas, tomatoes, and string beans. Bordered by a scenic cranberry bog, a small pond, and conservation land, this is an ideal spot for picnicking after a day of exploration.

If you visit the Cape in the winter, you won't have any trouble finding quiet places to explore. In the summer, it's not as easy, but it can still be done, especially midweek. Even on a weekend in the middle of the tourist season, I've been able to find a combination of solitude and beauty by rising at dawn and canoeing on one of the mist-shrouded ponds or walking along the coast. I love to watch a beach come to life, and the surf, no matter what its size, is always a delight to the eye.

In the Area

All numbers are within area code 508.

Cape Cod Chamber of Commerce: 362-3225

Falmouth Chamber of Commerce: 548-8500

Ashumet Holly Reservation and Wildlife Sanctuary (East Falmouth): 563-6390

Peters Pond Campground (Sandwich): 477-1775

Tony Andrews Farm (East Falmouth): 548-5257

Barnstable County Fair: 563-3200

The Trustees of Reservations (information number): 921-1944

Wampanoag Tribal Council (Mashpee): 477-0208

Cahoon Museum of American Art (Cotuit): 428-7581

Bibliography

Bates, Betty M., and Cynthia H. Krusell. *Marshfield, A Town Village 1640–1990.* Marshfield Hills: Historical Research Associates, 1990.

Beston, Henry. *The Outermost House.* New York: Ballantine Books, 1928.

Bickford, Walter E., and Ute Janik Dymon. *An Atlas of Massachusetts River Systems, Environmental Designs for the Future.* Amherst: University of Massachusetts Press, 1990.

Bourne, Russell. *The Red Kings Rebellion.* New York: Oxford University and Atheneum Publishers, 1990.

Cadbury, Henry. "Society of Friends," from *World Book Encyclopedia.* Chicago: Field Enterprises Education Corporation, 1963.

Caswell, Clark, and Cushman Cowan, et al. *North Middleborough Looks Back,* 1976.

Crawford, Michael J. *A History of Natick, Massachusetts.* Natick: Natick Historical Commision, 1978.

Dupuis, William O. *Historic Sites of Boylston,* Vol. VII. Boylston: Boylston Historical Commission, 1979.

Horstman, Judith. "North River" from *Yankee Magazine.* Dublin, New Hampshire, May 1990.

Howe, Henry F. *Prologue to New England.* New York: Farrar and Rinehart, 1943.

The Junior League of Boston, Inc. *Along the Coast of Essex County.* Prides Crossing, Massachusetts: J.W. Murray & Associates, 1970.

Levine, Miriam. *A Guide to Writer's Homes in New England.* Cambridge: Apple-wood Books, 1984.

Moon, William Least Heat. *Blue Highways*. New York: Ballantine Books, 1982.

Peru History Committee. *A Bicentennial History of Peru, 1771–1971*. Peru, Massachusetts, 1971.

Romaine, Mertie. *History of the Town of Middleboro, Massachusetts, 1905–1965*, Vol. II. New Bedford: Reynolds-De Walt Printing, Inc., 1969.

Rowlandson, Mary. *The Narrative of the Captivity and Restoration of Mrs. Mary Rowlandson*. First printed 1682. The National Bicentennial Edition, by Robert Diebold and the Town of Lancaster, Massachusetts, 1975.

Southeastern Regional Planning and Economical Development District. *Middleborough Historical Preservation Plan*. 1989.

Stowe, Harriet Elizabeth Beecher. *Old Town Folks*. Edited by Genry F. May. Cambridge: Harvard University Press, Belknap Press, 1966.

Thoreau, Henry David. *Walden and Other Writings*. Edited by Joseph Wood Kruch. New York: Bantam Books, 1962.

Thoreau, Henry David. *The Natural History Essays*. Salt Lake City:

Gibbs Smith, Publisher, Introduction copyright 1980.

Tilden, William. *History of the Town of Medfield, Massachusetts, 1650–1886*. Boston: George H. Ellis Publisher, 1887.

The Trustees of Reservations. *A Guide to Properties of The Trustees of Reservations*. Beverly, Massachusetts.

Weston, Thomas. *History of the Town of Middleborough, Massachusetts, 1669–1905*. Boston & New York: Houghton Mifflin, 1906.

West Brookfield Historical Commission. *Historical Site Tour of West Brookfield*. (pamphlet)

Index

Agassiz Rock, Manchester, 61
Air Plum Island, 68
Andrews, Tony, Farm, Falmouth, 114, 115
Apple Inn B&B, Ashfield, 22
Ashfield, 18–19
Ashfield Fall Festival, 22
Ashfield Inn, 19, 22
Ashumet Holly Reservation and Wildlife Sanctuary, East Falmouth, 107–108, 115
Assawompsett Pond, Middleboro, 87

Bacon Free Library (museum), South Natick, 71
Barnstable County Fair, Mashpee, 113, 115
Barre, 45
Barton Cove, Gill, 30
Bayberry Meadow Tree Farm, Princeton, 59
beaches
　Crane Beach, 63
　Duxbury Beach, 103, 104
　South Cape Beach, 113
Bears Maple Distillery, Whately, 32
Becket Arts Center, 12
bed and breakfasts, see inns
Berkshires, 1–13
Bittersweet Farm, Duxbury, 105
Black Pond Nature Preserve, 97–98
Blue Meadow Farm, Montague, 32

Blueberry Hill Farm, Mount Washington, 12
Bolton Spring Farm, Bolton, 59
Book Bear, West Brookfield, 36, 46
Boyden Brothers Sugarhouse, Conway, 15
Boylston, 49, 50–51
bridge (steel and wooden truss), Conway, 21
Bridge of Flowers, Shelburne Falls, 20
bridges
　bridge (steel and wooden truss), Conway, 21
　Bridge of Flowers, Shelburne Falls, 20
　Burkville Covered Bridge, Conway, 16
　Powder Point Bridge, Duxbury, 102
　Pratt Bridge, 81, 82
Bridgewater, 82–83
Broadmoor Wildlife Sanctuary, Natick, 72–73, 78
Brookfield Orchards, Brookfield, 46
Brookledge Sugarhouse, Whately, 32
Bryant, William Cullen, Homestead, Cummington, 11, 13
Buckland, 19–20
Buckland Historical Society, 22
Bucksteep Manor B&B, Washington, 12

Burkville Covered Bridge,
  Conway, 16
Buzzards Bay, 89

Cahoon Museum of American
  Art, Cotuit, 111, 115
canoe and boat rental
  Foote Brothers Canoe Rental,
    Ipswich, 63, 68
  Gate 43 (Quabbin Reservoir),
    40
  New England Outdoor Center,
    Millers Falls, 30, 32
Canterbury Farm B&B, Becket, 12
Cape Cod, 106–115
Castle Hill, Ipswich, 62–63, 68
cemeteries
  Highland Cemetery, Dover, 77
  Ipswich cemetery, 65
  Nemasket Hill cemetery,
    Middleboro, 85
  Pine Nook Cemetery, 26
  Sherborn cemetery, 74
  Stockbridge Cemetery, Norwell,
    97
  Titicut Parish Cemetery, 80, 81
  Winslow Cemetery, Marshfield,
    100
Centennial House B&B,
  Northfield, 32
Cervelli Farm, Rochester, 88

Chalet d'Alicia, Peru, 5, 12
Chapelbrook Reservation,
  Ashfield, 17–18
Charles River, 69–78
Christmas tree farms
  Covered Bridge Christmas Tree
    Farm, Conway, 22
  Glendon Tree Farm, Windsor,
    12
  Kip's Christmas Tree Farm,
    New Braintree, 45, 47
  Lone Maple Farm, Princeton,
    59

Nourse Farms, Hatfield, 25, 32
  Riverbrook Christmas Tree
    Farm, Whately, 32
  Tree-Berry Farm, Scituate, 105
churches and meetinghouses
  Congregational Church,
    Phillipston, 44
  First Congregational Church,
    Middleboro, 85
  First Congregational Church,
    Princeton, 54
  First Parish Church, Cohasset,
    96
  Long Plain Friends
    Meetinghouse, Lakeville, 91
  Saint Stephen's Church,
    Cohasset, 96, 104
  St. John's Episcopal Church,
    Ashfield, 18
cider, see fruits and vegetables
Clarence and Esther Warner farm,
  Sunderland, 32
Clarkdale Fruit Farm, Deerfield,
  33
Cohasset, 96–97
Colonel Isaac Barre Restaurant
  and Meetinghouse Tavern,
  Barre, 45
Congregational Church,
  Phillipston, 44
Connecticut River, 22–33
Conway, 15–17, 21
Cook's Maple Products,
  Worthington, 3, 13
Corners Grocery, Worthington, 2
Cotuit, 111–112
Country Cricket Village Inn &
  Restaurant, Worthington, 2,
  13
Country Store, Petersham, 42
country stores
  Corners Grocery, Worthington,
    2
  Country Store, Petersham, 42
  Hardwick General Store, 39–40

Index

Old Creamery Grocery, Cummington, 9
Petersham Country Store, 42
Covered Bridge Christmas Tree Farm, Conway, 22
Cranberries, 85-86
Crane Beach, 63
Crane Museum, Dalton, 6, 12
Cummington, 9–11
Cumworth Farm, Cummington, 11–12, 13

Dalton, 6
Daniel Webster Wildlife Sanctuary, 101
Days Inn, Middleboro, 92
Deerfield, 27–28, 32
Deerfield Inn, 32
Deerfield River, 8, 28
Dorothy Francis Rice Sanctuary, 5–6
Dover, 77
Duxbury Beach, 103, 104
Duxbury, 102–103

E & J Scott Orchards, Ashfield, 22
Eayrs, Ted, antiques, 80
Edaville Railroad, South Carver, 86–87, 92
Elliot Laurel Reservation, 44–45
Elm Bank Reservation, 70–71
Essex, 61
Essex Shipbuilding Museum, 61, 68

fairs and festivals
  Ashfield Fall Festival, 22
  Barnstable County Fair, Mashpee, 113, 115
  Hardwick Fair, 38, 47
  Hot Air Balloon Festival, Worthington, 3
  Jacobs Pillow Dance Festival, Becket, 12
  King Richard's Faire, Carver, 87, 92
  Marshfield Fair, 105
  Topsfield Agricultural Fair, 65, 68
  Wampanoag Indian powwow, Mashpee, 109
Fairview Farms, Whately, 32
Falmouth, 110, 113–114
Field Memorial Library, Conway, 15–17
First Congregational Church, Middleboro, 85
First Congregational Church, Princeton, 54
First Parish Church, Cohasset, 96
Fisher Museum, Petersham, 43
Foote Brothers Canoe Rental, Ipswich, 63, 68
forests, see parks
Franklin milestone, West Brookfield, 35
French King Motor Lodge, Millers Falls, 32
fruits and vegetables (see also Christmas tree farms, sugar houses)
  Bittersweet Farm, Duxbury, 105
  Blueberry Heaven Blueberry Farm, Washington, 13
  Blueberry Hill Farm, Mount Washington, 12
  Blue Meadow Farm, Montague, 32
  Bolton Spring Farm, Bolton, 59
  Brookfield Orchards, Brookfield, 46
  Cervelli Farm, Rochester, 88
  Clarence and Esther Warner farm, Sunderland, 32
  Clarkdale Fruit Farm, Deerfield, 33
  Cumworth Farm, Cummington, 11–13

fruits and vegetables (*continued*)
  E & J Scott Orchards, Ashfield, 22
  Fairview Farms, Whately, 32
  Goodale Orchards, Ipswich, 62, 68
  Greenwood Farm, Northfield, 31–33
  Hartman's Herb Farm, Barre, 45, 47
  Jonathan's Sprouts, Rochester, 88–89, 92
  Lookout Farm, Natick, 77, 78
  Meadowbrook Orchards, Sterling, 59
  Mohawk Orchards, Shelburne Falls, 22
  Nashoba Winery Orchard, Bolton, 59
  Nourse Farms, Whately, 25, 32
  Quonquont Farm, Whately, 32, 33
  Ray & Marilyn Wiley, Washington, 13
  Red Apple Farm, Phillipston, 47
  Ripka's Farm, South Deerfield, 33
  Tee-Zee Farm, Hatfield, 33
  Tony Andrews Farm, Falmouth, 114, 115
  Tree-Berry Farm, Scituate, 105
  Warner Farm, Sunderland, 33

gardens
  Bridge of Flowers, Shelburne Falls, 20
  Stritch Sculpture Garden, Hinsdale, 6, 12
  Tower Hill Botanic Garden, Boylston, 49–50, 59
glacial potholes, Shelburne Falls, 20
Glendale Falls, Middleton, 6
Glendon Tree Farm, Windsor, 12
Goodale Orchards, Ipswich, 62, 68
Gray's Sugarhouse, Ashfield, 19

Great Quittacas Pond, Middleboro, 87
Greenwood Farm, Northfield, 31–33
Gurnet Inn, Marshfield, 104

Hardwick, 38–41
Hardwick Fair, 38
Hardwick General Store, 39–40
Harrington Farm Country Inn, Princeton, 59
Hartman's Herb Farm, Barre, 45, 47
Harvard Forest, Petersham, 43
Hatfield, 25
Hell's Blazes Restaurant, Middleboro, 92
Hickory Hill Ski Touring Center, Worthington, 3, 13
Highland Cemetery, Dover, 77
Highland Sugarbush Farm, Ashfield, 22
Hinsdale, 6
Historic Deerfield, 27–28, 32
historic homes
  Castle Hill, Ipswich, 62–63, 68
  John Whipple House, Ipswich, 65
  King Cesar House, Duxbury, 103, 104
  Oak Grove Farm, Millis, 76
  Peak House, Medfield, 76–77
  Richardson House, Millis, 76
  Thomas W. Waters Memorial Heard House, Ipswich, 65
  William Cullen Bryant Homestead, Cummington, 11, 13
  Winslow House, Marshfield, 101–102, 104
Hot Air Balloon Festival, Worthington, 3

inns, bed and breakfasts, hotels and resorts
  Apple Inn B&B, Ashfield, 22
  Ashfield Inn, 19, 22

Index

Bucksteep Manor B&B, Washington, 12
Canterbury Farm B&B, Becket, 12
Centennial House B&B, Northfield, 32
Chalet d'Alicia, Peru, 5, 12
Country Cricket Village Inn & Restaurant, Worthington, 2, 13
Cumworth Farm, Cummington, 11, 13
Days Inn, Middleboro, 92
Deerfield Inn, 32
French King Motor Lodge, Millers Falls, 32
Gurnet Inn, Marshfield, 104
Harrington Farm Country Inn, Princeton, 59
Kimballs Motor Inn, Cohasset, 104
Long House B&B, Becket, 12
Mattapoisett Inn, 89, 90, 92
Merriams (The) B&B, Conway, 22
Red Lion Inn, Cohasset, 105
Salem Cross Inn, West Brookfield, 36, 47
1797 House, Buckland, 20, 22
The Stall B &B, Peru, 12
Suisse Chalet, Middleboro, 92
Sunnyside Farm B&B, Whately, 32
Swift River Inn, Cummington, 9, 13
Winsor House Inn, Duxbury, 104
Winterwood, Petersham, 43, 47
Worthington Inn, 3, 12
Ipswich, 65
Ipswich River, 63–64

Jacobs Pillow Dance Festival, Becket, 12
John Whipple House, Ipswich, 65
Jonathan's Sprouts, Rochester, 88–89, 92

Kimballs Motor Inn, Cohasset, 104
King Cesar House, Duxbury, 103
King Richard's Faire, Carver, 87, 92
Kingman Tavern Historical Museum, Cummington, 9–10, 13
Kip's Christmas Tree Farm, New Braintree, 45, 47
KOA Campground, Middleboro, 92

lakes, see ponds
Lone Maple Farm, Princeton, 59
Long House B&B, Becket, 12
Long Plain Friends Meetinghouse, Lakeville, 91
Lookout Farm, Natick, 77, 78
Lowell Holly Reservation, Mashpee, 110–111

Manchester, 61
maple sugar, see sugar houses
Marion, 90
Maritime Museum, Cohasset, 96
Marshfield, 99–102
Marshfield Fair, 105
Marty's Riverside Restaurant, Shelburne Falls, 20
Mashpee, 107–110
Mashpee Pond, 109–110
Mashpee River, 112–113
Mashpee River Reservation, 112
Mashpee Wampanoag Indian Museum, 108
Massachusetts Audubon Society (South Shore), 104
Mattapoisett, 89–90, 92
Mattapoisett Inn, 89, 90, 92
Mattapoisett Historical Society and Carriage House, 90, 92

Meadowbrook Orchards, Sterling, 59
Memorial Hall Museum, Deerfield, 28
Merriams (The) B&B, Conway, 22
Merrimack River, 67
Middleboro, 83–85
Middleboro Historical Museum, 83–84, 92
Middlefield, 5–6
Milepost Tavern Restaurant, Duxbury, 105
Millis, 75–76
Mohawk Orchards, Shelburne Falls, 22
Montague, 29
Mt. Esther Sugarhouse, Whately, 32
museums (see also historic homes)
  Bacon Free Library (museum), South Natick, 71
  Cahoon Museum of American Art, Cotuit, 111, 115
  Crane Museum, Dalton, 6, 12
  Essex Shipbuilding Museum, 61, 68
  Fisher Museum, Petersham, 43
  Kingman Tavern Historical Museum, Cummington, 9–10, 13
  Maritime Museum, Cohasset, 96, 104
  Mashpee Wampanoag Indian Museum, 108
  Mattapoisett Historical Society and Carriage House, 90, 92
  Memorial Hall Museum, Deerfield, 28
  Middleboro Historical Museum, 83, 92
Myles Standish homesite, Duxbury, 104
  Monument, 104
  Reservation, South Duxbury, 103

Nantucket Sound, 114
Nashoba Winery Orchard, Bolton, 59
Ned's Point, Mattapoisett, 90
Nemasket Hill cemetery, Middleboro, 85
Nemasket River, 84–85
New Braintree, 45–46
New England Outdoor Center, Millers Falls, 30, 32
Noanet Woodlands, Dover, 77
Noon Hill Reservation, 76
Norris Reservation, 98–99
North Meadow Common, Petersham, 42–43
North Middleboro (Titicut Green), 79–80
North River, 98–100
Northfield Mountain Recreation and Environmental Center, 30, 32
Notchview Reservation, Windsor, 9, 12
Nourse Farms, Whately, 25, 32

Oak Grove Farm, Millis, 76
Old Creamery Grocery, Cummington, 9
Old Indian Meetinghouse, Mashpee, 109
Old Town Hill Reservation, 66
Oliver Mill picnic area, Middleboro, 84, 85

Parker River, 65–66
Parker River National Wildlife Refuge, 66–67, 68
Parker River Trading Post, Rowley, 65
parks, reservations, sanctuaries, and wildlife areas
  Ashumet Holly Reservation and Wildlife Sanctuary, 107–108, 115

Index

Barton Cove, Gill, 30
Black Pond Nature Preserve, 97–98
Broadmoor Wildlife Sanctuary, Natick, 72–73, 78
Chapelbrook Reservation, Ashfield, 17
Daniel Webster Wildlife Sanctuary, 101
Dorothy Francis Rice Sanctuary, 5–6
Elliot Laurel Reservation, 44–45
Elm Bank Reservation, 70–71
Harvard Forest, Petersham, 43
Lowell Holly Reservation, Mashpee, 110–111
Mashpee River Reservation, 112
Noanet Woodlands, Dover, 77
Noon Hill Reservation, 76
Norris Reservation, 98–99
North Meadow Common, Petersham, 42–43
Northfield Mountain Recreation and Environmental Center, 30, 32
Notchview Reservation, Windsor, 9, 12
Old Town Hill Reservation, 66
Oliver Mill picnic area, Middleboro, 84, 85
Parker River National Wildlife Refuge, 66–67, 68
Peters Reservation, 74–75
Plum Island, 66–67, 68
Pratt Farm Conservation Area, Middleboro, 85
Raccoon Hill Wildlife Management Area, 41
Shattuck Reservation, 76
Shipyard Park, Mattapoisett, 89–90
Standish (Myles) Reservation, South Duxbury, 103–104
Stavros Reservation, 62
Sugarloaf State Park, Deerfield, 25
Swift River Reservation, 45
Wachusett Reservoir, 51–52
Wachusett Meadows Wildlife Sanctuary, 55–56, 59
Whitney Thayer Reservation, 97
Windsor State Forest, 9, 12
World's End Reservation, Hingham, 94–95
Peak House, Medfield, 76–77
Peru, 3–5
Peters Reservation, 74–75
Peters Pond Campground, Sandwich, 111, 115
Petersham, 41–43
Petersham Craft Center, 43, 47
Phillipston, 43
Pine Nook Cemetery, 26
Plum Island, 66–67, 68
Plymouth, 104
ponds
  Assawompsett Pond, Middleboro, 87
  Great Quittacas Pond, Middleboro, 87
  Mashpee Pond, 109–110
  Pottapaug Pond, 40
  South End Pond, Millis, 75–76
  Wakeby Pond, Mashpee, 109–110
Pony Mountain, Ashfield, 17–18
Powder Point Bridge, Duxbury, 102
Pratt Farm Conservation Area, Middleboro, 85
Pratt Bridge, 81, 82
praying woman statue, South Natick, 72
Princeton, 54–57
Purington Maple, Buckland, 22

Quabbin MDC Visitor Center, 47
Quabbin Reservoir, 34–47

Quinapoxet River, 52–54
Quinnetucket II, 31
Quonquont Farm, Whately, 32, 33

Raccoon Hill Wildlife
    Management Area, 41
Ray & Marilyn Wiley farm,
    Washington, 13
Red Apple Farm, Phillipston, 47
Red Bucket Sugar Shack,
    Worthington, 2, 13
Redemption Rock, 57–58
Red Lion Inn, Cohasset, 105
reservations, see parks
restaurants
    Colonel Isaac Barre Restaurant
        and Meetinghouse Tavern,
        Barre, 45
    Country Cricket Village Inn &
        Restaurant, Worthington, 2, 13
    Hell's Blazes Restaurant,
        Middleboro, 92
    Marty's Riverside Restaurant,
        Shelburne Falls, 20
    Milepost Tavern Restaurant,
        Duxbury, 105
    Rossi's Restaurant, Millis, 78
    Salem Cross Inn, West
        Brookfield, 36, 47
Rice, Dorothy Francis, Sanctuary,
    5–6
Richardson House, Millis, 76
Ripka's Farm, South Deerfield, 33
Riverbrook Christmas Tree Farm,
    Whately, 32
rivers
    Charles River, 69–78
    Connecticut River, 22–33
    Deerfield River, 8, 28
    Ipswich River, 63–64
    Mashpee River, 112–113
    Merrimack River, 67
    Nemasket River, 84–85

North River, 98–100
Parker River, 65–66
Quinapoxet River, 52–54
South River, 16
Swift River, 41
Taunton River, 80–82
Ware River, 40
Westfield River, 8–9
Rochester, 88, 91
Rossi's Restaurant, Millis, 78

St. John's Episcopal Church,
    Ashfield, 18
Saint Stephen's Church, Cohasset,
    96, 104
Salem Cross Inn, West Brookfield,
    36, 47
Salmon Falls Artisans Showroom,
    Shelburne Falls, 20, 22
Sawyer Memorial Library,
    Boylston, 50–51
Scott, E & J, Orchards, Ashfield,
    22
Seasons Gift Shop, Dover, 77
1797 House, Buckland, 20, 22
Shattuck Reservation, 76
Shaw Hudson House, 22
Shelburne Falls, 20
Sherborn, 73–74
Shipyard Park, Mattapoisett,
    89–90
South Cape Beach, 113
South Duxbury, 103
South End Pond, 75–76
South Natick, 71, 72
South Natick Dam, 71, 72
South River, 16
South Shore Art Center,
    Cohasset, 104
The Stall B&B, Peru, 12
Standish (Myles) Reservation,
    South Duxbury, 103
    homesite, 104

Index

Monument, 104
Stavros Reservation, 62
Stockbridge Cemetery, Norwell, 97
Stritch Sculpture Garden, Hinsdale, 6, 12
sugar houses and maple products
  Bears Maple Distillery, Whately, 32
  Boyden Brothers Sugar House, Conway, 21
  Brookledge Sugarhouse, Whately, 32
  Cook's Maple Products, Worthington, 3
  Cumworth Farm, Cummington, 11–12, 13
  Fairview Farms, Whately, 32
  Gray's Sugarhouse, Ashfield, 19
  Highland Sugarbush Farm, Ashfield, 22
  Mt. Esther Sugarhouse, Whately, 32
  Purington Maple, Buckland, 22
  Red Bucket Sugar Shack, Worthington, 2, 13
Sugarloaf Mountain, 25–26
Sugarloaf State Park, Deerfield, 25
Suisse Chalet, Middleboro, 92
Sunnyside Farm B&B, Whately, 32
Swift River, 41
Swift River Inn, Cummington, 9, 13
Swift River Reservation, 45

Taunton River, 80–82
Tee-Zee Farm, Hatfield, 33
Thomas F. Waters Memorial Heard House, Ipswich, 65
Titicut Green, 79–80
Titicut Parish Cemetery, 80, 81
Tony Andrews Farm, Falmouth, 114

Topsfield, 65
Topsfield Agricultural Fair, 65, 68
Tower Hill Botanic Garden, Boylston, 49–50, 59
The Trustees of Reservations (information), 115
Tree-Berry Farm, Scituate, 105

Wachusett Reservoir, 51–52
Wachusett Meadows Wildlife Sanctuary, 55–56, 59
Wachusett Mountain, 49–50, 57, 59
Wahconah Falls, 6–7
Wahconah Stables, Hinsdale, 12
Wakeby Pond, 109–110
Wampanoag Indian powwow, Mashpee, 109
Wampanoag Tribal Council, 109, 115
Ware River, 40
Warner, Clarence and Esther, farm, Sunderland, 32
Warner Farm, Sunderland, 33
Waters, Thomas W., Memorial Heard House, Ipswich, 65
Webster, Daniel, 100–101
  Wildlife Sanctuary, 101
West Brookfield, 36
Westfield River, 8–9
Whipple, John, House, Ipswich, 65
Whitney Thayer Reservation, 97
wildlife areas, see parks
Wiley, Ray & Marilyn, farm, Washington, 13
William Cullen Bryant Homestead, Cummington, 11, 13
Willowdale Mill, Hamilton, 64–65
Windsor, 6–8
Windsor State Forest, 9, 12
Windsor Dam, Ware, 36–37

Winslow Cemetery, Marshfield, 100
Winslow House, Marshfield, 101–102, 104
Winsor House Inn, Duxbury, 104
Winterwood inn, Petersham, 43, 47

World's End Reservation, Hingham, 94–95
Worthington Inn, 3, 12
Worthington, 2–3

Yankee Candle Company, Deerfield, 28, 32